THE YOKE MADE EASY

Alfred Doerffler

Publishing House
St. Louis   London

Meditations and prayers for the sick, convalescents, and invalids who are seeking comfort, encouragement, hope, and peace in the Gospel of Jesus Christ, the Great Physician of souls and Savior of all mankind.

Concordia Publishing House, St. Louis, Missouri
Concordia Publishing House Ltd., London, E. C. 1

MANUFACTURED IN THE UNITED STATES OF AMERICA

Library of Congress Cataloging in Publication Data

Doerffler, Alfred, 1884-
    The yoke made easy.

    1. Sick — Prayer-books and devotions — English.
2. Meditations. 3. Sight-saving books. I. Title.
BV4910.D63 1975   242'.4   75-2344
ISBN: 978-0-7586-1834-4

Come unto Me, all ye that labor and are heavy laden, and I will give you rest. Take My yoke upon you, and learn of Me; for I am meek and lowly in heart; and ye shall find rest unto your souls. For My yoke is easy, and My burden is light. — *Matt. 11:28-30.*

Is there some problem in your life to solve,
    Some passage seeming full of mystery?
God knows, who brings the hidden things to light.
    God holds the key.

Is there some door closed by the Father's hand
    Which widely opened you had hoped to see?
Trust God and wait; for when He shuts the door,
    He holds the key.

Is there some earnest prayer unanswered yet
    Or answered not as you had thought 'twould be?
God will make clear His purpose by and by.
    God holds the key.

CONTENTS

Our Burden-Bearing God

Cast thy burden upon the Lord, and He shall sustain thee. —*Ps. 55:22.*

It is worth our time and effort to restudy the familiar statements of the Bible. Here is one which we have known from childhood days. As years have gone by, it has lost some of its meaning and significance for us. Every time we worry, we are ignoring this promise of our Lord.

"Cast thy burden upon the Lord." With that God admits that we have burdens. He does not tell us as we struggle through life and face the hardships of the week that all these burdens are a hallucination of the mind. They are real. But these burdens should not become worries.

God does not only admit that we have burdens, but He likewise concedes that they are too heavy for us to bear alone. He knows that they will crush us unless He gives us the strength to carry them.

We are to cast *all* our burdens upon the Lord, also the lifelong burdens and afflictions and the long-drawn-out sicknesses. These want to crush a family. There is no escape from the daily sameness. Under such conditions invalids often become despondent.

They become weary of being helpless. Without God and faith in the love of God such burdens crush us.

We are to cast all burdens upon the Lord, also the imaginary burdens. Thousands of people are borrowing trouble. They worry about things that never come to pass. They always see shadows on the walls, scarecrows in the fields, and ghosts in the gloomy halls of life.

Whatever our burdens may be, God asks us to cast them upon Him. There is no other way of ridding ourselves of them. We cannot remove them, our friends cannot take them away, and the devil will not.

> Other refuge have I none;
> Hangs my helpless soul on Thee.

"And He shall sustain thee" is the promise God makes to us all. If we believe this, we need not worry; in fact, we have no right to worry, no more than the lily of the field, the sparrows on the housetop, and the ravens, which have no barns. By our worries we offend God, we sin. Worry shows that we lack confidence in our Lord.

Above all, we are to cast upon the Lord the burden of our sin. Sin robs us of hope; and where there is no hope, there is no peace of heart and mind. God emphatically declares that we have sinned. Yes, God tells us that sin will completely crush us unless it is removed. The burden of sin is taken away only through Jesus Christ, who went with the sin of the world through life to the cross and paid the price of our redemption by suffering and dying for us. If we cling to Jesus, trust in Him as our Savior, then day after day our sins are removed.

If we cast this burden of sin and all the burdens of this life upon the burden-bearing God, we have nothing to worry about. Day after day we shall receive power from the Almighty to sustain us, and we shall dwell in peace and safety today, tomorrow, in death, and throughout eternity.

Prayer

We are Thy people, gracious Lord, for Thou hast called us out of darkness through the Gospel into the marvelous light of Thy Son Jesus Christ. As our Lord and heavenly Father Thou hast promised to keep us. Thou art our Shepherd, our Strength, and our Stay. Therefore I come to Thee with the burdens of my life, asking that Thou wouldst remove them if it be Thy will. Above all, I ask Thee to take away all my sins and blot them out forevermore. Make me trustful and confident. Fretfulness and worry want to rob me of peace and contentment. Lord, Thou knowest how the worries and the cares of this life do beset me. Teach me to trust in Thee as a child trusts its mother. Forgive me where I have doubted

Thy promises. Strengthen my faith and give me courage to carry on.

Lord, I need Thee every hour; be with me. Watch over each one in this household. Bless those that take care of me. I ask this for the sake of Him who has given His life that I may have peace, Christ Jesus, my Lord. Amen.

God Knows You by Name

I have called thee by thy name; thou art Mine. — *Is. 43:1*

"Life is a chance," many tell us. To such, life is like a roulette wheel, which stops at random, at any number, without plan, without purpose, and without reason. Those who believe that life is aimless and planless deny God and His divine providence.

Others are not ready to rule God out of existence. Nevertheless, they believe that God is so much occupied with the big things of the universe that He cannot be concerned about little me. Herein is found no consolation.

The Scriptures, however, offer us a great comfort. They tell us that God knows each and every one of us by name. He thinks about us. God tells us in His Word that He has inscribed our names in the Book of Life. We are personally known to God. He is acquainted with our problems, our difficulties, and our troubles. He also knows of our sins, our many transgressions. He knows of our doubts and our fears. Therefore, in tender compassion He has given us His Word to instruct and comfort us. He gives us the assurance: "I have called thee by thy name."

What does God say to you and me as He calls to us, "Thou art Mine"? He claims us as His own because Christ has redeemed us, not with gold or silver, but with His holy, precious blood. Christ has bought us with a price. Every believer's name is written in the Book of Life. God loves us with an everlasting love in Christ Jesus. He is with us day after day in sickness and in trouble.

To understand the call of God, we must know His voice. He speaks to us in and through His Word. Let us heed His voice and abide in His presence.

Lying upon the sickbed, we should derive endless comfort from this assurance: "Thou art Mine"; for God does not forsake His own.

Prayer

Heavenly Father, Thou hast called me out of darkness into the light of Thy grace and art my Refuge and Strength in these days of trouble and distress. I seek Thee. In tender mercy look upon me and deliver me. I come mindful of my many transgressions. I am unworthy of Thy grace. But Thou art full of tender compassion in Christ Jesus. Cleanse me from every sin. Accept me as Thine own. Keep me in Thy grace.

Be with each and every one in this household and bless us all. Fill us with peace and with joy. Let us delight in Thy Word. Into Thy hands I place myself for the Savior's sake. Amen.

Prayer Opens the Door

Knock, and it shall be opened unto you. — *Luke 11:9*

Jesus urges us to pray. We are not merely to ask now and then, but to be persistent in prayer. Therefore he says, "Knock." "Which of you," He argues, "shall have a friend and shall go unto him at midnight and say unto him, Friend, lend me three loaves; for a friend of mine in his journey is come to me, and I have nothing to set before him? And he from within shall answer and say, Trouble me not; the door is now shut, and my children are with me in bed; I cannot rise and give thee. I say unto you, Though he will not rise and give him because he is his friend, yet because of his importunity" — because he insists — "he will rise and give him as many as he needeth."

If you and I will give beggars and solicitors something merely to get rid of them, how much more will God give us what we need if we plead and beg. Therefore Jesus says: "Knock, and it shall be opened unto you."

The Lord invites you to come to Him with all your problems, cares, and worries. You can come at all times, knocking at the door in prayer, and He will open.

On the one hand, we are to knock at the door and ask for help for ourselves. We are to make known to Him our needs. We are to seek His help both for body and soul. Physical hunger we feel at once. Many of us, however, do not long for spiritual food for the soul. However, we are to seek first God's help for the needs of the soul, and He will likewise give us our daily bread to support and sustain our body.

On the other hand, we are to knock at the door and ask for others. The Bible speaks of making intercessions for all men; that is, we are to pray for others. Our prayers should be all-embracing. The world is our field of prayer. One moment we can pray for some missionary in India, pleading with God to encourage him in the performing of his difficult task, and the next moment we can pray for some lost soul living next door.

Whether we pray for ourselves or for others, Christ Jesus gives us the assurance: "It shall be opened unto you." The Lord hears our prayers. How encouraging to us in the days of trouble and sickness! This promise fills us with hope. This promise teaches us to pray diligently and then to wait upon the Lord with confidence. Let us continue instant in prayer. Let us pray always.

Prayer

Gracious and merciful Father, I come to Thee as the very present Help in trouble. Thou hast promised to open the door to me as I pray. Thou hast given me the blessed assurance that Thou wilt abide with me when every other comfort fails. Lord, I put my trust in Thee. I beseech Thee, forsake me not. I am unworthy of Thy divine grace; I am mindful of my many sins. But, Lord, according to Thy grace blot them out and remember them no more. Create in me a clean heart and renew in me a right spirit that I may daily seek Thee in prayer and live in communion with Thee.

Bless our home. Make us all realize that Thou art ever ready to hear our prayers and dost love us with an everlasting love. Protect us from all dangers of body and soul.

Give unto me peaceful days and restful nights. Let not the cares and worries of life rob me of hope. I ask this in the name of Him who taught us to pray: "Our Father who art in heaven." Amen.

Praying with Confidence

And this is the confidence that we have in Him, that, if we ask anything according to His will, He heareth us. — *1 John 5:14.*

The best way to ascertain whether prayer is answered is to try it. The testimony of thousands of Christians bears witness to the fact that God hears us as we call upon Him in the day of trouble. For this reason the Scriptures urge us to be diligent in prayer. Since most of us are daily facing vexing and trying problems, we are often discouraged and disheartened. Yet we have at our very door a power that can accomplish mighty things for us. Therefore St. John writes: "This is the confidence that we have in Him, that, if we ask anything according to His will, He heareth us." To pray successfully, we must pray with confidence.

To pray with confidence, we must be certain that we are addressing the right person. The Bible tells us to pray to the Lord of heaven and earth, who has revealed Himself in the Scriptures. God alone is able to hear our prayers, and to Him we should go. If I am sick, I call in a physician and not a lawyer. The lawyer may offer me legal advice, yes, he may even give me some hints on health. But when I am critically ill, I go to some reputable physician and let him examine me and prescribe something for me. If I want my prayers to accomplish something, I must go to God, the true and living God, who has spoken to me through the divine Word.

I can approach my Lord with confidence because He has asked me to pray. Through the psalmist He tells you and me: "Call upon Me in the day of trouble; I will deliver thee." Through these words God assures us an audience; He tells the believers that He is a loving Father, and therefore we can "with all boldness and confidence ask Him as dear children ask their dear father." That is why John says, "He heareth us."

To pray with confidence, we must furthermore be certain that we are addressing our Lord God in the right manner. "This is the confidence that we have in Him, that, *if we ask anything according to His will,* He heareth us."

To pray according to His will, we must pray in humility of heart. The man or the woman who struts into the presence of the Lord, proud and haughty, finds the door closed. The Scriptures say: "A broken and a contrite heart, O God, Thou wilt not despise."

To pray in the right manner, we must also submit ourselves to the Lord's will. We are not to dictate to Him. We are not to come into His presence and tell

Him *how* He must answer our prayer. As loving children we are mindful of the fact that our Lord is all-wise and therefore in His superior wisdom knows what is best for us. For this reason we add in submission of spirit, "If it be Thy will."

To pray in the right manner, we should also pray for something definite. We are not merely to say, "Lord, help everybody," but we are to ask the Lord to send His divine blessings upon John and to be a Strength to Mary in her trouble. We are to pray for individual souls. We are to pray for the pastor that the Lord may give him the courage to proclaim the Word in its truth and purity. We are to acquaint ourselves with the special problems of our congregation and then earnestly to pray that the Lord may guide and direct all to do His will. If we pray definitely, we shall soon discover that God is answering our prayers. This will convince us that our prayers accomplish much.

To pray in the right manner, it is essential that we pray with a forgiving heart. Jesus stresses this when He says: "When ye stand praying, forgive if ye have aught against any, that your Father also which is in heaven may forgive you your trespasses. But if ye do not forgive, neither will your Father which is in heaven forgive your trespasses." God does not hear the prayers of those who are nursing a grudge, who are spiteful and unforgiving. As long as we are filled with malice and revenge, the door will be closed to us.

Above all, to pray in the right manner, we must pray in Jesus' name. The Savior says: "Whatsoever ye shall ask the Father in My name, He will give it you." We are God's beloved children only through Christ Jesus. If we ignore the Savior, we cannot expect to see the Father's friendly face. We must come with Jesus. I cannot walk into any bank and expect it to cash my check. I can go only to a bank that knows me or that knows you if you take me there. We are reconciled only through Jesus Christ, and therefore we must come with Him and in His name to God.

To pray with confidence, we must also be certain that we are addressing the Lord God about the right things. When I know that I am asking for the right thing, then I can be certain that He hears me. Now there are certain things which positively oppose the will of God. In His Word He tells me that they are sinful. They are harmful to my body and dangerous to my soul. On the other hand, I know that there are certain things that God desires very much. He wants all mankind to be saved. "As I live, saith the Lord God, I have no pleasure in the death of the wicked, but that the wicked turn from his way and live." Therefore you and I should pray for the unconverted.

If you know of anyone who is stubborn and will not confess his transgressions, pray for him.

Then God wants us to pray for spiritual things. He wants you and me to pray for ourselves that we may grow in grace and the knowledge of our Lord and Savior Jesus Christ. We are to ask God to fill us with patience in the days of sickness, with cheerfulness amid adversities, with faith when every earthly comfort fails.

If we pray in the right manner for the right things to the Lord, our God, then we can have the confidence that "He heareth us."

Prayer

Lord, heavenly Father, in the name of Jesus Christ, my Savior, I approach Thee today, beseeching Thee to let Thy grace and Thy mercy rest upon me. Assure me of Thy divine presence. In Thy tender mercy forgive me all my sins with which I have grieved Thee, and fill me with that blessed peace which comes to all believers. Let me grow in grace and in the knowledge of my Lord and Savior Jesus Christ.

Lord, I ask Thee not only for myself. I beseech Thee to bless also those who live in this household, to bless my friends that come to cheer me, to bless the physician who calls upon me. I ask Thee to bless my church that it may serve as a beacon light to all the weary and to the troubled of this world. I ask Thee to bless my minister that in season and out of season he may proclaim the glorious Gospel that

Christ Jesus came into the world to save sinners. Bless the boys and girls of the church that they may become wise unto salvation through Thy blessed Word. Grant that the parents of this community may rear their children to the glory of Thy name. Lord, have mercy upon me and keep me day after day cheerful, humble, and confident. I ask this in Jesus' name. Amen.

Prayers Which Accomplish Much

The effectual, fervent prayer of a righteous man availeth much. —*James 5:16.*

God's children of all ages have prayed. Only as we become careless and indifferent about our soul's salvation do our prayers become mere form and finally cease altogether.

Prayer accomplishes much. In answer to our prayers God gives us strength to face the trials of life and to withstand the temptations of Satan.

Should prayer, however, accomplish much, it must be fervent. Now a fervent prayer is a heartfelt prayer. It rises from the depth of our innermost soul and is stripped of all pretense.

Such prayer is made thoughtfully. We do not hasten to the throne of God and make our requests at random. We consider first what we are going to say. If you would call upon the governor of your state, you would give much thought to the things that you intended to say. You would not let your words fall from your lips thoughtlessly. In prayer you are calling upon the King of kings.

If we pray thoughtfully, then naturally we shall pray definitely. To pray merely in a general way for the welfare of all mankind is not praying fervently. We should have something specific in mind. We know of men and women who are sick. We have friends who are indifferent to the Gospel call. We know that our church has missionaries in foreign fields. If we pray for these by name, we shall pray more fervently.

Such definite prayer makes us confident. We can check up on our prayers and know whether or not they have been heard. Finding that they are actually answered gives us greater confidence in the future. It fills us with the unshaken conviction that God does answer prayer.

Fervent prayer is made by the righteous. There are two classes of righteous people: those who are righteous, or good, in the sight of men and those who are righteous in the sight of God. That which makes us righteous before men is outward goodness, respectability, and decency. Such as are righteous only before men become self-righteous and self-satisfied, believing that they are good enough in themselves even before God. Their prayers are not effectual but an abomination unto the Lord.

That which makes us righteous before God is the removal of our sin. But sin can be removed only through the blood of Jesus Christ. The righteous in the sight of God have been cleansed and washed from all their sins and are reconciled to God through our Lord and Savior.

Such righteous persons pray in the name of Jesus. "Whatsoever ye shall ask the Father in My name, He will give it you." The believer makes his approach through Christ; for God is his Father only in Christ Jesus.

Such as pray in Jesus' name fervently accomplish much to the glory of God and the welfare of immortal souls.

Prayer

In the name of our Lord Jesus Christ, who has purchased us with His holy, precious blood, I approach Thee, O Lord, heavenly Father, beseeching Thee to hear my prayer. I need Thee every hour to protect and to shield me against sin, which constantly assaults my soul. I need Thee to protect me against the forces of unbelief, which seek to rob me of my faith, which is built upon Thee. I need Thee in these days of sickness and affliction. I come to Thee because I know that all things are possible with Thee.

Thou hast so often upheld me when every other help has failed. Therefore I put my trust in Thee. In the long night watches I seek Thee, and in the daytime I depend upon Thy goodness. Bless each and every one in this home with an unshaken faith, which confidently trusts that all will be well as long as Thou art with us. I ask all this for the sake of Him who has promised to be with us always, even unto the end of the world, Christ Jesus, my Lord. Amen.

Useless Praying

Ye ask and receive not because ye ask amiss. —*James 4:3*

People of all nations pray. God commands us to come to Him when we pray. He promises those who seek Him: "I will deliver thee." Yet some pray amiss, James tells us in his epistle. Which are such useless prayers?

Thoughtless praying is useless. "When ye pray, use not vain repetitions, as the heathen do; for they think that they shall be heard for their much speaking," Matt. 6:7. Merely saying prayers with the lips is not praying. Such praying is done mechanically, merely by force of habit. Therefore it is useless.

Christless praying is useless. "Verily, verily, I say unto you, Whatsoever ye shall ask the Father in My name, He will give it you," John 16:23. We must approach God through Christ Jesus. Sin has separated us from our Lord. Only through Christ Jesus is sin removed; for He has suffered upon the cross and shed His holy, precious blood that we might be cleansed and washed from all our sins. Only because of Jesus Christ, God, our Father, is reconciled. Christless prayers are an affront to God. They accomplish nothing. They are useless.

Dictatorial praying is useless. Sometimes men and women want to tell God what to do and how He should answer prayer. We are to remember that God is the Lord of heaven and earth, who knows all things. Moreover, we are nearsighted, shortsighted. God has greater wisdom and a better understanding of all things than we. Therefore we should leave the "how" to God, saying, "Lord, if Thou be willing."

Asking for foolish and hurtful things is useless. The mother of the sons of Zebedee prayed: "Grant that these my two sons may sit, the one on the right hand and the other on the left hand, in Thy kingdom." Jesus did not grant this prayer, but said: "Ye know not what ye ask." That mother had a perfect right to ask that the Lord save her sons James and John, but to beseech Him to give them honor places in heaven was preposterous. The thing that we ask for may not appear to us as foolish or harmful, but God knows that the granting of this or that petition may lead to our bodily or spiritual ruin. Therefore again we are to add, "Lord, if Thou be willing."

Praying without faith is useless. "All things, whatsoever ye ask in prayer, believing, ye shall receive," Matt. 21:22. Doubt and unbelief defeat the very purpose of prayer. We should feel confident that God is answering our prayer and therefore thank Him immediately. This we do by adding the amen, which means, "It shall be so."

Selfish praying is useless. That which should prompt us to pray is the glory of God and the welfare of immortal souls, our own as well as others. To seek our interests at the expense of others is not pleasing to God. Such praying is useless.

If our prayer is not to be useless and futile, then we must pray according to the will of God, in the name of Jesus, and with a believing heart.

Prayer

Lord God, gracious and merciful, I seek Thy throne through my Lord Jesus Christ, asking for Thy divine blessings both of body and soul. Thou art acquainted with all my needs. Nothing is hidden from Thee. Therefore I place all my problems before Thee, asking that Thou wouldst guide and help me as Thou seest fit for my welfare in time and eternity.

If I have grieved and offended Thee with my

transgressions of Thy holy will, graciously blot out all my sins and cleanse me through the precious blood of Jesus Christ, my Redeemer.

Graciously bless this home and dwell in our midst as our heavenly Father, keeping us in the only saving faith, the faith in Christ Jesus. Bring us all at last to the eternal kingdom, where all problems will be solved and where fulness of joy will abide forevermore. I ask this for Jesus' sake. Amen.

The Power of Prayer

He shall call upon Me, I will answer him. —*Ps. 91:15*

Doctors Walton and Cockroft accomplished the astonishing feat of splitting the atom. Tremendous claims had always been made as to what would happen when this feat would be accomplished. In a tumbler of water there is supposed to lie enough power to drive any vessel across the Atlantic Ocean and back.

In the spiritual world there is likewise a power that is tremendous. It can produce rain and cause the winds to cease. This is the power of prayer.

Prayer can accomplish much. God says so. Prayer can lift trouble from our shoulders; for God says: "Call upon Me in the day of trouble, and I will deliver thee." Again: "Whatsoever ye shall ask the Father in My name, He will give it you."

God's children have experienced this to be true. When the children of Israel, under the leadership of Moses, were in the wilderness, the Amalekites fought against them. Moses placed Joshua at the head of the army, while he himself went to the top of a mountain to pray. The Bible records that Israel prevailed while Moses held up his hands in prayer; but the moment he would let them down and ceased praying, Amalek won. For this reason Aaron and Hur got a stone upon which Moses could sit, and then each of them took hold of Moses' arms and held them up while he prayed. This was done until the going down of the sun and until Joshua had defeated Amalek.

During the persecution of the first Christians at Jerusalem, King Herod had Peter arrested and imprisoned. While Peter was in prison, the church made prayer without ceasing before God. And behold, an angel of the Lord came to Peter one night in prison and commanded him to rise up quickly; and the chains fell from his hands. Then the angel said to Peter: "Gird thyself and bind on thy sandals." He did so. The angel went out of the prison, and Peter followed him past the first and the second watch and finally out of the city. The prayers of these first Christians accomplished this release.

But in our time this power of prayer is seldom used. We are living in a prayerless age. We cannot deny this. The church is not a praying church. If the prayers in the public services go beyond 2 and 3 minutes, we become impatient. We are wondering how soon the amen will announce the end of the prayer.

Many homes are not praying homes. We are told that the mother of Wesley retired each day for an hour to some solitary place to pray. She was the mother of 17 children and certainly was a busy house-wife. Nevertheless, she gave a full hour each day to the Lord. Where are fathers and mothers today who give so much time to prayer? The day is begun, the week is often lived through, without much earnest praying.

True, we have our prayers. Nevertheless, much of this is mechanical. It is done by rote. Many have not dared as yet to cease making their formal prayers. They still believe that the Lord is God and that, if they do not recognize Him in some way, He may send His judgment upon them.

Yet prayer accomplishes much, and by ignoring it, we are closing the door upon the mightiest force we have as God's people and as a Christian church and as a nation. We have not because we ask not; we have not because we ask amiss. God has told us how to pray — according to His will, in the name of Jesus, with firm confidence.

Above all, let us remember that Christ has made God-pleasing prayer possible through His sacrifice on the cross. He has reconciled us to God. Being justified through the blood of Jesus Christ, we now have access to the throne of grace. In all our troubles, then, let us go to God in prayer, and we shall find immediate help in every trouble.

Prayer

Lord, with heavy heart and troubled mind I come to Thee as the only Helper in my distress. Thou art acquainted with all the trials and afflictions of my life and art able to help me to the uttermost. Therefore I seek refuge in Thee. In the past Thou hast been my Stay and my Strength; continue also for today and for tomorrow.

I confess that I have not always prayed to Thee, O Lord, nor praised Thee for Thy goodness and mercy nor worshiped Thee with all my heart and with all my soul. Forgive me all my sins and blot them out with Christ's precious blood. Give me grace to trust in Thee. Strengthen my faith in Thy promises. Make me hopeful, cheerful, and confident. Let Thy continual presence and Thy divine forgiveness remain with each and every one of us who abide in this home. I ask this in the name and for the sake of Jesus Christ, my Lord. Amen.

Thirty-two Thousand Promises

For all the promises of God in Him are yea and in Him amen, unto the glory of God by us. —*2 Cor. 1:20*

There are more than 32,000 promises in the Bible in which God pledges to give us certain gifts and assures us positive help to carry on as we go through life and as we face trouble. These promises God fulfils for us day after day. Paul confidently asserts that "all the promises of God in Him are yea and in Him amen"; that is, they shall come to pass as certainly as God Himself lives.

As you go through the Scriptures reading these promises of God, you will be encouraged and heartened and made to feel that all is well because God is with you. He sustains you by giving you what you need for the support and wants of the body. He offers you forgiveness of sins, peace of heart and mind. He fills you with an undying hope in Christ Jesus, who has suffered on the cross, risen from the dead, ascended on high, and is coming again to receive us to Himself.

If God has pledged all these things to us, then certainly we have no right to doubt and to question the goodness and the mercy of our Lord. We are to glorify

His name by confidently believing His promises.

Prayer

Lord, strengthen Thou my faith so that I may hold fast to the many promises that Thou hast given to me. Let me not doubt that Thou art a help in the day of trouble and that Thou art the One that upholds me in my distress. Behold my anguish and my pain, and help me. As I toss restlessly upon my bed, quiet Thou my nerves and fill me with peace by removing every worry that vexes and tries me. Forgive me all my sins and keep me in Thy divine love and grace for Jesus' sake. Amen.

The Faith That Counts

Abraham believed God, and it was counted unto Him for righteousness. —*Rom. 4:3.*

The faith that counts, the faith that saves, is faith in Jesus Christ. Jesus Himself declared: "He that believeth on Me hath everlasting life."

The Christian faith is built on Christ, not on ourselves nor on people nor on government; but it is built on Jesus Christ, the Son of God, who came into the world to seek and to save that which was lost. Abraham had such a faith, a faith that believed the promise of God that in his Seed all the nations of the earth shall be blessed. Therefore the text significantly says: "Abraham believed God, and it was counted unto him for righteousness."

If we have this faith in Christ Jesus, our sin is not counted against us. Every human being has sinned. Yes, day after day even we who believe are transgressing against God's holy law. We sin in thought, word, and deed. These sins offend our Lord. These sins make us guilty before God. Therefore our conscience accuses us, especially in the days when trouble comes into our lives.

Now there is only one satisfactory way in dealing with sin, namely, through Jesus Christ. He blots out all our sins through His holy, precious blood. Believing this, cleanses and purifies us and removes all our transgressions. David said: "Blessed are they whose iniquities are forgiven, whose sins are covered." The debt has been removed from God's books and is no longer counted against us.

This assurance is given to me through the Gospel. For this reason I need not fear the judgment of God; for hiding behind Christ, I am saved, I am at peace with God.

Having this faith in Christ Jesus, I am righteous before God because all my sin is blotted out. "Abraham believed God, and it was counted unto him for righteousness." The Scriptures do not say that Abraham was innocent. God in His Word rather tells us that we all have sinned and fallen short of the glory of God. Those who believe in Jesus Christ never claim to be innocent. From their lips do not fall expressions such as these: "I have never done any wrong. I thank God that I am not like others." Yet the Christian takes God at His word that Christ has removed all his sins. And this faith of his that holds fast to Christ, who has cleansed us from all sins, makes him righteous. Legally nothing stands against the believer, because Jesus has paid the full price of His redemption.

Such believers, made righteous through Jesus Christ, are justified. Justified means acquitted because another has paid the sin debt. This "another" is Jesus Christ. In the courts of God the believer stakes his all upon his Savior, and "there is therefore now no condemnation to them which are in Christ Jesus." However, we must always remember that the believer is not acquitted on his own merits or because of his splendid character. He is acquitted, or justified, solely and alone because he stakes his all upon Jesus Christ, who has redeemed him, a lost and condemned creature.

This is the faith that counts. This faith brings us into the right relationship with our heavenly Father.

We need not despair as long as we hold fast to the Gospel, which assures us of the forgiveness of all our sins in Christ Jesus and therefore promises us life everlasting.

In the days of trouble and sickness, as we search our hearts more seriously than in the days of health, let us in faith look up to Jesus Christ and find in Him hope and certainty. Believing in Him gives us the blessed assurance that, though we have sinned, we are saved, that we are heirs of eternal life. We are at peace with God even as we bear the burdens of life and endure great suffering and pain in our sickness and affliction. Knowing that we are the dear children of our heavenly Father enables us to bear patiently the trials of the day.

Prayer

My faith looks up to Thee, gracious Savior; for through Thee alone I am certain of my salvation. I have nothing to fear, even though I pass through the deep, dark valleys of suffering and pain, because Thou art with me. Since Thou hast redeemed me, certainly Thou wilt not forsake me as I lie upon this bed of anguish and pain. Let Thy Word and Thy promises strengthen my faith. Let me have the blessed assurance that Thou wilt guide me and fill me with hope and cheerfulness. Remove all rebellious thoughts from my heart. Teach me to trust Thy promises.

In Thy grace and mercy forgive me wherever I have sinned against Thee. Remember not the sins of my youth nor my many shortcomings of the past. I have not always loved Thee, O Lord, with all my heart. Today these sins come to my remembrance; but I come to Thee that Thou mayest wash me whiter than snow through Thy precious blood.

Bless our home with Thy divine presence and keep us faithful to Thy holy Christian church that we may share with all the faithful the glories of that eternal kingdom where all the redeemed will worship Thee as the Lamb that was slain for our eternal redemption. Amen.

No Slough of Despond

Out of the depths have I cried unto Thee, O Lord. Lord, hear my voice; let Thine ears be attentive to the voice of my supplications. —Ps. 130:1-2.

We all have cried out of the depths to the Lord. We all have staggered and stumbled. Many have fallen into the pit of trouble. Sickness and pain vexed us, and anxiety and worry gripped our hearts. In such moments we have wrung our hands in agony and spent sleepless nights, wondering whither these troubles would lead us. Truly, these are depths that try our souls.

But this is not the depth of which the psalmist is thinking. Sin has cast him into the deep and dragged him down into the mire. We, too, have sinned. We have not walked all the day with the Lord nor glorified His name. We have not prayed from morning till night nor thought our thoughts after Him. Sin puts us where we ought not to be. Sin makes us guilty and ashamed. Adam therefore hid himself in the Garden after he had transgressed.

It is impossible for us to get out of this depth if we are depending upon our own strength. I can pull at my bootstraps and wear myself out doing so and yet not lift myself one-sixteenth of an inch from the ground. So it is impossible for you and for me to lift ourselves out of the depth of sin. We cannot by character, we cannot by one good turn a day, we cannot by any tears that we shed lift our souls out of the depth of sin. This we must realize.

The psalmist knows that he cannot save himself, yet he is not despairing. Neither should you and I lose hope. With a triumphant conviction that nothing can shake, the sacred penman declares: "But there is forgiveness with Thee."

To forgive means to cancel. Sin has been canceled with the precious blood of Jesus Christ and not by ourselves. Christ hands us the canceled bill upon which is written: "I, even I, have blotted out thy transgressions and will remember them no more." This assures us of perfect peace and fills us with a glorious hope.

Who is this man crying unto the Lord? I search in vain to find the name of him who has written this psalm. God wants you and me to make this psalm our own. It is you and I who cry out of the depths unto the Lord. As we do, peace and hope and strength fill our hearts. God lifts us out of the depths, embraces us with His loving arms, that we might be His own for time and eternity.

Prayer

Lord, Thou art my Refuge and my Strength, my Light and my Salvation. I seek Thee. In my helplessness I come to Thee. My sins sorely distress me, but I hasten to Thine everlasting arms, seeking forgiveness. Lord, if Thou shouldst mark iniquity, I should not be able to stand. But in Thee is forgiveness through the precious blood of Jesus Christ. Wash me thoroughly from all my sins and heal me from all my diseases. Give me grace to believe Thy promises. Let my days be restful and bless me with sleep throughout the night. I ask all this because of Him who in His great love has given His life that I might live eternally, Christ Jesus, my Lord. Amen.

Teach Us to Pray

And it came to pass that as He was praying in a certain place, when He ceased, one of His disciples said unto Him, Lord, teach us to pray. *—Luke 11:1.*

Jesus was a man of prayer. His disciples were greatly impressed with His much praying. When He was about to heal the sick, He prayed; before He fed the hungry multitude, He first prayed; when He was perplexed, He went into the mountain to pray; before He entered upon His great passion, He prayed earnestly in the Garden.

As the disciples observed their Lord in prayer, they were filled with a desire to pray. Therefore one of them asked Jesus, "Lord, teach us to pray." This same desire should fill our hearts, especially as we note that prayer accomplished so much for those disciples who had learned from Jesus to pray. We, too, should sit at Jesus' feet in spirit and learn from Him to pray; for He has told us in His Word how to pray.

1. Jesus tells us to pray *in His name.* "Verily, verily, I say unto you, Whatsoever ye shall ask the Father in My name, He will give it you," John 16:23. We have sinned and therefore have no right to come

into the presence of God with our blackened hearts, our sullied lips, and our stained hands. Only through Jesus Christ is sin removed. He came into the world for this purpose, that He might cleanse us from our sins and make us acceptable to His Father in heaven. Therefore the believer must approach God in prayer through Christ; for God is our gracious heavenly Father only in Christ Jesus, our Savior.

2. Jesus tells us to pray *believingly.* "All things, whatsoever ye shall ask in prayer, believing, ye shall receive," Matt. 21:22. We are to believe confidently that God hears our prayers. I may send a letter to the President of the United States which may never reach him personally. His secretaries open the mail and perchance will not consider my letter important enough to give it to the busy President. But with God it is quite different. I am to believe that He hears my prayers; for so He has promised.

I am to believe that God can do what I ask. He is almighty. I must believe that God can change the course of things to answer my prayer. True, God does not always do so, because as the All-Wise He knows that certain things for which I ask are harmful to me. But I should be confident that He can remove mountains if it need be. He can do the humanly impossible.

3. Jesus tells us to pray *forgiving others.* "When ye

stand praying, forgive if ye have aught against any," Mark 11:25. Someone has hurt us, someone has grieved us. So we become embittered, yes, spiteful and revengeful. These grievances we are to bring to God in prayer. Thereby, by telling God, we relieve our pent-up feelings. But as we make these things known unto God, we should pray, "Forgive them." We dare not remain unforgiving in the presence of our Lord.

4. Jesus tells us to pray *behind shut doors.* "Thou, when thou prayest, enter into thy closet; and when thou hast shut thy door, pray to thy Father which is in secret," Matt. 6:6. We are living in a noisy age. This makes it rather difficult to concentrate. So many things distract our minds. Therefore Jesus tells us to enter into some room alone, shut the door, and pray. We should try to get away from everything and get composed and quiet our nerves. As we do this, we shall enter into prayer unhurried and put our whole mind upon our petitions and requests.

5. Jesus tells us to pray *abiding in His Word.* "If ye abide in Me, and My words abide in you, ye shall ask what ye will, and it shall be done unto you," John 15:7. We cannot pray in the right manner if we dishonor the Lord with false doctrine and ungodly living. While indifferent to truth and indifferent to morals, we cannot pray as we ought. Only if we be-

lieve God's revealed Word, if we live the Christian way, can we pray in spirit and in truth. If a man comes to my door and says: "I know that you are a liar, but please give me a dollar for a night's lodging," I am afraid he will not get the dollar. If you dishonor God by not believing His Word nor living a Christian life according to it, then you cannot expect an answer to your prayers.

6. Jesus tells us to pray *putting first things first.* This He does Himself in the Lord's Prayer, Matt. 6:9-13; Luke 11:2-4. In this model prayer He puts the spiritual things first. In fact, they take up by far the greater part of the prayer. In this prayer taught by the Lord we have six petitions pertaining to the soul and only one which asks for blessings for the body. The first three ask that the Lord send spiritual blessings upon us. We ask that He may grant us grace to hallow His name by believing His Word and living a Christian life; that His kingdom may come and the Christian church grow; that His good and gracious will be done and we be strengthened and preserved steadfast in His Word and faith unto the end. In the last three petitions we ask that He would guard our souls against evils, removing our sins, giving us the strength to resist the temptation of the devil, preserving us from an ungodly death, and taking us out of this vale of tears to Himself in heaven. Only

41

one petition asks for bread and all that we need for the want and the support of this body. Thus Jesus urges us to seek first the kingdom of God and His righteousness.

7. Jesus tells us to pray *always*. "Men ought always to pray and not to faint," Luke 18:1. The door to prayer is always open day and night. In health and in sickness we may come to God in prayer. Our thoughts should always turn heavenward.

Thus as we sit at Jesus' feet, we learn of Him that prayer is a vital part of our life and that we ought to pray diligently and always.

Prayer

Lord, I beseech Thee to teach me to pray with a believing heart. Give me grace to hold fast to Thy promises, which say: "Ask, and it shall be given you." Keep me daily in touch with Thee through prayer. Remove all distracting thoughts and worries and cares that want to hinder me in my prayers.

I ask Thee to bless me by healing my body and by cleansing my soul. However, I do not ask only for myself, O Lord, but for each and every one who lives in this household. Yes, I ask also for my friends that they may be kept steadfast in the faith. I ask Thee to protect Thy Christian church and to keep it faithful to its mission of preaching the Gospel that many may be saved. Wherever there is a soul in great distress, reveal unto it Thy saving Word and fill it with hope and the blessed assurance that underneath are the everlasting arms of the Almighty that keep it.

I thank Thee, gracious Savior, that Thou hast taught me to pray, above all, that Thou dost delight in hearing my prayers and dost not weary as I continue day after day pleading for help and for mercy. Amen.

The Grace Wherein We Stand

Therefore, being justified by faith, we have peace with God through our Lord Jesus Christ; by whom also we have access by faith into this grace wherein we stand and rejoice in hope of the glory of God. — *Rom. 5:1-2.*

We are standing in grace. What is this grace in which we stand? It is the transcending grace of God, which has found a way to bring lost sinners into His favor, namely, through the atoning sacrifice of Jesus Christ. This grace wherein we stand is the renewing grace, which makes us new creatures, who are reborn into the kingdom of our Lord and Savior. Standing in this grace, we Christians become a unique people. Simon Peter says by divine inspiration: "Ye are a chosen generation, a royal priesthood, an holy nation, a peculiar people."

Paul tells us that, justified by faith, we are standing continually in the grace of God. A new joy and satisfaction takes hold of our hearts. We can never live again in the gloom and hopelessness of un-regenerated people.

Standing in this grace, we have been *justified* before God by faith. "Justified" means that we have been acquitted, not because we are innocent, but because Jesus Christ for us and in our place has paid for our sins with His death on the cross.

We are justified *by faith*. We must look up to Jesus Christ as our Lord and Savior, believing that He has died for us. We look to Him for our salvation. We stake everything on Him. As we are justified by faith, nothing can condemn us. We are continually covered with the righteousness of Jesus Christ.

Standing in this grace, we have peace with God. Our conscience is at ease. We are not afraid of the Lord; for He is our loving Father in Christ Jesus. Paul tells us that we can hardly define this peace when he declares that it passes all understanding.

Standing in this grace, we have peace over against the accusing conscience. In this grace we are undis-turbed by the fact that we must stand in the courts of God to face the Judgment. The believer knows the verdict; for there is no condemnation for them that believe.

Standing in this grace, we have peace as we face

the troubles of life. No matter how dark the night in the heavens, God's stars of love are shining. In all our troubles we know that underneath are the everlasting arms of a forgiving Lord.

This peace is ours because of Jesus' blood. God spared not His own Son, but gave Him up for us all. The blood of Jesus Christ cleanses us from all sin.

Standing in this grace, we enjoy the favor of God. We have access into this grace, and as dear children we can speak with all boldness and confidence to our heavenly Father. We can come to Him in prayer and know that He is eager and anxious to hear us. In all our troubles, with all our problems, amid all our difficulties, we can daily speak to the Lord. On our sickbed we have much time. Often when the nights are long, let us occupy ourselves diligently with prayer.

Standing in this grace, we rejoice in the hope of the glory of God. As we pass through the valley of tears and trouble, we can look forward to the day of glory, when God shall wipe away all tears from our eyes. This glory of heaven is so great that Paul declares: "I reckon that the sufferings of this present time are not worthy to be compared with the glory which shall be revealed in us."

Standing in this grace, then, we have no reason to worry, much less to become despondent. The Lord is with us. He will supply us day by day with the necessities of life and give us sufficient strength each day to bear the burdens that rest upon us. Above all, daily He will forgive all our sins and give us the blessed assurance of life everlasting. Nothing can separate us from the love of God because, being justified by faith, we have peace with Him through our Lord Jesus Christ.

Prayer

Lord Jesus, adorable Savior, Thou hast brought me into this grace wherein I stand through Thy suffering and death on the cross. Grant that I may continue day by day in this grace and find true peace, satisfaction, and hope amid my troubles and afflictions of life.

Thou hast loved me unto death. Grant that I may always love Thee. In my distress and pain remind me of Thy Passion, of the great agony which Thou hast endured to redeem me. Amid my worries and cares let me know that Thou wilt not forsake me, who has not spared Thy life to make me Thine own. Have mercy upon my soul, fill me with peace, give unto me the joy of my salvation.

Come into our home and bless each and every one of us. Fill us with contentment. Let not the cares of life make us irritable and peevish. Make us more diligent in prayer and teach us patiently to wait on Thee, believing that Thou wilt hear us.

We ask this of Thee because Thou art our Lord and our Savior, our Redeemer and our King. Amen.

The Anchor Holds

> There failed not aught of any good thing which the Lord had spoken unto the house of Israel; all came to pass. — *Joshua 21:45.*

"Change and decay in all around I see," sings the great hymnist Henry Lyte. However, some things never fail, and some things never change. The everlasting promises of God stand sure, and God Himself is eternally the same. In the days of sickness and trouble we want to remember this. It is certainly an amazing statement that Joshua pens at the close of his life when he declares: "There failed not aught of any good thing which the Lord had spoken." Yet it is gloriously true. Which are some of these promises of God that never fail?

"When thou passest through the waters, I will be with thee." This life holds in store for us troubles, sickness, sorrow, misfortune, and death. God, however, gives us the assurance when these things come into our lives: "I will be with thee." The cable may give; but the anchor holds.

"All things work together for good to them that love God." This life holds many mysteries. We look through a glass, darkly, and cannot understand why many things have befallen us. But God assures us that all will turn out for our good. He says "all things," the big as well as the insignificant things, the successes as well as the troubles. All things will work together for good, not merely measured by today, but by eternity; not merely the things pertaining to the body, but above all the things that have to do with our soul.

"The blood of Jesus Christ, His Son, cleanseth us from all sin." Sin condemns. Sin dirties our soul. We need cleansing. The guilt must be removed. Someone has said:

> I wish that there were some wonderful place,
> Called the Land-of-beginning-again,
> Where all mistakes and all our heartaches
> And all of our poor, selfish griefs
> Could be dropped like a shabby old hat at the door
> And never be put on again.

We can be cleansed. There is for us a Land-of-beginning-again. Jesus Christ came into the world to pay the price of our redemption, and He has done so with His holy, precious blood. In Christ we can begin anew. We can enjoy daily the forgiveness of all sins. What comfort! What peace!

Make your petitions large. Jesus tells us: "Ask, and it shall be given you." We are to ask for the great and the small, for ourselves and for others. In days of health and in days of sickness, Jesus promises: "It shall be given you." We are not to be timid, but continually to petition the Lord and make all our wants and desires known to Him. He may not always give us cake, but He will never give us a stone. He will always give us those things that we need for the support and wants of our body and above all the spiritual blessings, which are essential to our soul's salvation.

"In My Father's house are many mansions; if it were not so, I would have told you." Shall we live again? Shall we see those who are gone into eternity? Here is the promise, and the promises of Jesus are yes and amen; they are certain. Heaven is our home through Christ Jesus, our Lord.

These are some of the many promises that are given us by our Lord, and as we look back into our yesterdays, we also must acknowledge with Joshua that none of His promises have failed us, but that they have all been fulfilled. Therefore we can look hopefully into the future, confident that the Lord will not fail us.

Prayer

Lord, fulfill Thy promises to me today and lift me out of my distress. I have been sorely tried, and my spirit is greatly depressed. The vexations of the day have been many, and the troubles are being heaped in great numbers upon me. Whither shall I go but to

Thee, who art the Almighty and who art able to save unto the uttermost?

Forgive me, O Lord, forgive me all my sins. Let me start anew today with Thy divine guidance and protection. Remember not my transgressions of yesterday. Wash me thoroughly through Jesus Christ, my Savior.

Show me Thy loving-kindness and Thy tender mercies and give me a restful day.

Into Thy divine hands I place myself and all my household for the sake of Him who has purchased that perfect peace of heart and mind which passes all understanding, Christ Jesus, my Lord. Amen.

Our "Good-Lucker"

God is our Refuge and Strength, a very present Help in trouble. Therefore will not we fear. — *Ps. 46:1-2.*

Walking along the streets of Cairo, Egypt, I observed a man with an incense vessel, from which the smoke was rising. He entered a shop and soon filled the room with incense as he swung the incense burner to and fro. He likewise placed it upon the counter and the scales standing in the shop. I was informed that he was a "good-lucker." He was to bring business to the owner by burning incense in the shop. For this service he received a small coin and went on his way, while the owner felt confident that he would make a number of sales that particular day.

God, not luck, is our Fortress and our Strength. We are not to put our trust in omens, signs, and charms. These mean nothing. In the day of trouble our Lord is the one real Help and Refuge. If God be with us, who can be against us? Therefore we need not fear though the earth tremble beneath and though many evils surround us. God always knows a way out of every difficulty, and He can always protect His own.

We Christians therefore seek refuge with God. This we do through prayer. We believe that God can help to the uttermost. We feel confident that He can uphold us amid the swellings of Jordan and see us safely through every difficulty. Amid all our problems, be they sickness or affliction, misfortune or loss, we can rely upon Him for help. God can so turn the tide of things that we can escape with safety.

God is not only our Refuge in sickness and in trouble, but above all our Redeemer in our spiritual distress. He restores our soul and fills us with peace. He graciously forgives us our sins. He has sent His only-begotten Son into the world. Jesus has given His life on the cross that we might not perish. In Him we have a Lover of our souls, to whom we can go with our sins, with our doubts, and with our troubles.

He cleanses us and fills us with a glorious hope.

We do not know what the day has in store for us. We do know, however, that God is our Refuge and our Strength. He is a very present Help in trouble. He comes to our assistance at the time when help is most needed. Therefore we need not fear but can go forward unafraid.

Prayer

Heavenly Father, to Thee I come, asking that Thou wouldst guide and lead me through the day. I seek Thee as my Refuge and my Strength amid all the trials of my life. I put all my trust in Thee. Every morning Thou hast shown Thy loving-kindness to me anew and hast graciously protected me through the night. Even though I have sinned, Thou art merciful and hast forgiven all mine iniquities. Cleanse me again today and make my heart a temple wherein Thou canst dwell and abide. Bless Thou our home and our church and our nation. Grant that we all may recognize that Thou art the Giver of every good gift and art our gracious heavenly Father through Christ Jesus. Take me by the hand and direct me in all my ways. Keep me with this household in that saving faith which is in Christ Jesus, my Lord. Amen.

Walking in the Shadows

For our light affliction, which is but for a moment,
worketh for us a far more exceeding and eternal weight
of glory. — *2 Cor. 4:17.*

Throughout the greater part of his life Paul was
burdened with afflictions, but he sings. One never
hears a pessimistic note in his hymns of praise. There
are no discords in his heavenly harmonies. He even
rejoices in tribulation, "knowing that tribulation
worketh patience; and patience, experience; and experience, hope; and hope maketh not ashamed, because the love of God is shed abroad in our hearts
by the Holy Ghost, which is given unto us."

The Bible uses a number of expressions for the
afflictions which come into our lives. It speaks of
them as corrections. "Whom the Lord loveth He
chasteneth"; that is, He disciplines us as we go
through life.

Then the Bible speaks of afflictions as crosses,
something that we are suffering for Christ's sake. Not
all afflictions are crosses; for sickness, misfortune,
and troubles also come to those who are not Christians. The cross, however, is something that we
endure for the sake of our Lord. When a Christian

bears his afflictions in childlike faith, then these become a cross which the believer carries after his Savior cheerfully, patiently, and hopefully.

These afflictions are often grievous. Paul speaks of his as "a thorn in the flesh," something that irritates and gnaws at his body. Too often these afflictions make us afraid. As we look ahead, we become peevish or irritable because we think that God is not playing fair with us. We become nearsighted and short-sighted, forgetting the many blessings that lie behind us and the glory which is still before us.

Although the afflictions are grievous, nevertheless Paul calls them "light" because they have to do only with the present and with the material world. They are "for a moment," for the time being. After all, they do not rob us of the blessedness and the hope which the Gospel offers. They do not take from us the glory of heaven and the bliss of life everlasting. For this reason Paul stresses that they are "but for a moment."

True, often these afflictions last a lifetime. But in the hour-clock of eternity a lifetime is "but a moment." It seems long to us. When a mother waits for a message after an accident has happened to her boy, the minutes seem like days. But when the boy is off to a picnic, having a wonderful time, the day is but all too short. Looking forward to the eternal glory,

Paul says that these afflictions are light and for a moment, short lived.

Therefore we should look away from the earthly to the eternal. We are to focus our eyes on the unseen with all its glorious promises. Then shall we pile up for ourselves an eternal blessedness beyond all comparison. As we weigh our afflictions and put on the other scale the eternal glory, the glory of heaven far outweighs the troubles of our present life.

Should we, however, keep our eyes fastened on the glory that awaits us, then we must give attention to the promises which God has given us in His Word. The only one who can bear the trials and afflictions of life with cheerfulness is the believer. He knows that nothing can take from him the love of God which is in Christ Jesus, our Lord. Amid all the trials of life the Christian finds strength and hope in the Savior. That is why Paul says: "I can do all things through Christ, which strengtheneth me."

I do not believe that Charlotte Elliot would have written the beautiful hymn "Just as I Am" if she had not been an invalid. In her wheelchair she learned to know that life is not so bad nor so dreadful as long as Christ is in the heart. In her helplessness she writes:

> Just as I am, though tossed about
> With many a conflict, many a doubt,

Fightings and fears within, without,
O Lamb of God, I come! I come!

Prayer

Lord, my strength faileth me, and my soul is weary as I battle these days with the trials and problems of life. Therefore I come to Thee, gracious Lord, beseeching Thee to fill my heart with an unwavering faith, with a greater contentment, and a larger hopefulness. Give me grace to recognize that in Thee there is sufficient strength for each day. Impress upon my heart the truth that there is a never-ending glory for the people of God. May I learn to say with a believing heart, "Thy will be done," and recognize that Thy will is always a good and gracious will toward Thy people. Heavenly Father, I look through a glass, darkly, and cannot understand why these things have befallen me. Yet I am going to trust in Thee and hold to Thy promises, certain that Thou wilt fulfill them to me and also to our household. Bless me with a quiet, restful day; forgive me all my sins; strengthen my faith. I ask this for the sake of my Lord and Savior Jesus Christ, who has patiently borne the suffering on the cross to redeem me. Amen.

God's Abiding Presence

My presence shall go with you. —Ex. 33:14

As Christians we are traveling toward the Promised Land. Just how the road will wind and what difficulties and hardships we shall encounter as we travel on, we cannot tell. We shall meet with various experiences, joys and heartaches, pain and healing from pain. Much of the road is hidden from us.

Of one thing we are certain, however, the promise of God: "My presence shall go with thee." He is with us. He is with us through His Word. This is encouraging. This guarantees us protection and safety. When the brothers of Joseph, envious of the favor he enjoyed, sold him to the merchants going down to Egypt, God was with Joseph. Even though the young man was sent to the dungeon, he could not be harmed permanently. God turned everything to his good. At the close of his life he tells his brothers: "As for you, ye thought evil against me; but God meant it unto good, to bring to pass, as it is this day, to save much people alive."

God also promises to be with you in the days of trouble and sickness. Therefore seek Him in prayer. Thousands of men and women have discovered that God answers prayer and healed them.

God promises to give strength to the weak. Sometimes He permits us to endure affliction; but He also gives us the strength that enables us to bear the burden day after day. He never lets us be tempted and tried above that which we are able to endure.

"My presence shall go with thee." God abides with us. Others may leave, but God remains. Therefore we can be undismayed and unafraid. God's protecting arm shall shield us. Above all, God's gracious presence assures us eternal life.

Prayer

Lord, the way ofttimes is trying, and the days are lonely. Abide Thou with me with Thy love, with Thy strength, and with Thy peace. Alone I cannot carry on. Let Thy Word be a light unto my feet and a lamp unto my path. In the lonely hours of the night, watch Thou over me and protect me from every danger of body and soul. Remove every doubt that wants to come into my heart, and keep me steadfast in the faith unto the end. I ask all this in the name of Jesus, who has laid down His life to redeem us all. Amen.

On the Lone Trudge to Victory

I had fainted unless I had believed to see the goodness of the Lord in the land of the living. Wait on the Lord, be of good courage, and He shall strengthen thine heart; wait, I say, on the Lord. —*Ps. 27:13-14.*

It takes courage to face the great issues of life and remain hopeful. Fear, trouble, worry, anxiety, sin, are monsters that want to crush us. This holds true especially if our sickness and our afflictions run over a long period of time. The long trudge gets on our nerves. We become irritable. Alone we cannot face these problems of life and come forth victorious. This God never expects of us. He has promised to uphold us. For this reason we are admonished to wait upon the Lord and are given the blessed assurance that He shall strengthen our hearts. Too many have never learned the lesson of waiting upon the Lord in the day of adversity. They rather quit the Lord when tribulations come into their lives, thinking that God does not care for them. We cannot, however, expect any help from the Lord if we continuously ignore Him.

We are certainly strange creatures. In the day of prosperity we have no time for God, and in the day of adversity we have no use for God.

God has promised His presence and His aid to each and every one of His people. Not even a sparrow falls to the ground without His will. "Cast thy burden upon the Lord, and He shall sustain thee."

We know that these promises of God are true. Joshua confesses at the close of his life: "There failed not aught of any good thing which the Lord had spoken unto the house of Israel; all came to pass." Unless we believe in the goodness of the Lord, we simply shall faint by the way and go down into despair.

We wait upon the Lord with prayer. Prayer can accomplish more than anything else. But we are not a praying people. We are told that Martin Luther prayed for hours each day. The mother of the Wesleys withdrew every day from her household duties to devote an hour to prayer. James argues: "The effectual, fervent prayer of a righteous man availeth much."

We are to wait upon the Lord with confidence. We must believe that we shall see the goodness of the Lord fulfilled upon us. Therefore these prayers must rise from the heart. Prayer means nothing if merely uttered with the lips. We must believe that God will fulfill His promises to us. Too many, having prayed, are still doubting. Thereby they show lack of confidence and faith in the power of God to help.

With this confidence goes patience. We are to wait upon the Lord patiently. We are ready to wait when we deal with earthly things. We plant the seed and wait for it to grow. We know that it takes the seed a certain length of time to break through the earth and bud and flower. This same patience we should show toward God, confident that He answers our prayers.

If we wait upon the Lord, bringing to Him all our burdens and cares and sins, we shall discover the goodness of the Lord, His help, and His forgiveness. Daily we shall receive new strength. Therefore wait on the Lord, be of good courage, and He shall strengthen thine heart.

Prayer

Lord, gracious Father, I cannot live without Thee nor find any peace of heart and mind unless I come to Thee. Thou hast invited me to Thy throne room, even though I am unworthy, to make known all my wants and my needs. Thou art acquainted with my ways. Thou knowest my every thought. Ofttimes I have grieved Thee with my sins and vexed Thee with my transgressions. In Thy mercy, O Lord, forgive me; heal me through the precious blood of Jesus Christ, my Savior.

Give me sufficient strength for today to carry on. Fill my life with cheerfulness, with hope, and patience. Remove every rebellious thought. Into Thy divine hands I place myself, asking that Thou wouldst watch over me by day and by night, guarding and protecting me from the snares of sin and the doubts that Satan wants to put into my heart. Keep us all in Thy saving grace through Jesus Christ, our Lord. Amen.

Bucking the Winds

When even was come, the ship was in the midst of the sea and He alone on the land. And He saw them toiling in rowing; for the wind was contrary unto them. And about the fourth watch of the night He cometh unto them; . . . and He saith unto them, Be of good cheer; it is I; be not afraid. — *Mark 6:47-50.*

Life has often been compared to a voyage upon the trackless sea. The storms, the hidden shoals, the starless nights, are pictures of the trials, troubles, difficulties, and dangers which we meet on life's voyage. Today all is calm, and tomorrow it seems as though we would perish.

Sometimes the storms upon the sea are fascinating. Bucking the winds and the waves is a real sport as long as they are within bounds. They develop the strength of the swimmer and prove the seaworthiness of the ship. But sometimes storms arise that send fear into the hearts of men and drive even veteran sailors to their knees.

Every one must buck the winds of adversity as he goes through life. In such times some rise to real heights of Christian faith and sing and pray; others sink into the darkest unbelief and despair.

Bucking the winds of adversity alone, we soon are at our wit's end because doubt assails the heart. We will question the existence of God and wonder whether there is any plan, purpose, and aim as to our life. These misgivings become greater when we still believe in God, but question the justice of His ways with us. We see the ungodly prosper and the righteous suffer. We observe that God uses the wicked to chastise and correct the righteous. If we try to think this through without the Word of God, we shall soon be at our wit's end.

Coming to our wit's end, despair grips the soul, especially as our conscience accuses us of sin. Our conscience brings to our remembrance our indifference and our coldness in the days of health and prosperity.

But we shall be at our wit's end bucking the winds of adversity only until Jesus comes into our lives. He says to you and to me as He did to the disciples: "Be of good cheer; it is I; be not afraid."

We need not be afraid because Jesus is the Captain of our souls. After all, He controls the storms, He directs the winds, He stills the tempest. He is the

Rock that is higher than I. As long as He is the Captain of my soul, I need not doubt, much less despair.

As the Captain He gives me a compass, His Word. This compass of His Word always steers us aright, so that we go unerringly through life toward the glorious haven of heaven.

Since Jesus is the Captain of our souls, who guides us unmistakably through the Scriptures, we should trust in Him. To trust means to rely upon someone when everything seems to go contrary. If I trust a physician, I take his medicine even though I do not know what its ingredients are. If I trust a friend, I will hold to him even though some tell me he is faithless. As a Christian, then, I stake all upon Jesus Christ as my Lord and Savior.

If any of you are bucking the winds of adversity and it seems as though your ship is going down, take Jesus Christ, the Captain of your soul, into your life; cling to Him, trust Him, and He shall bring you safely to the eternal haven, where all trials end, where there is fullness of joy forevermore.

Prayer

Lord Jesus, Captain of my soul, pilot me safely through the tempestuous seas of this life. I know now what shall befall me tomorrow, what difficulties and trials I shall face. But Thou hast given me a compass and a chart in Thy Word. Give me the grace to use it to the saving of my soul. May I obey Thy Word! May I believe it and be unafraid and of good cheer, knowing that Thou wilt pilot me safely to eternal life!

Forgive me wherever I have offended Thee with my doubts and unbelief and sins. Keep me close to Thyself, Lord Jesus. Amen.

The Faith That Saves

Verily, verily, I say unto you, He that believeth on Me hath everlasting life. —*John 6:47.*

Jesus speaks here of the faith that saves. "He that believeth *on Me* hath everlasting life." Saving faith, then, stakes its all on Jesus Christ. This saving faith is not merely a knowledge concerning Jesus, that He was born, performed miracles, spoke parables, was crucified and died on Calvary. True, we must know that Jesus lived, died, and rose again. But there must be a plus.

Saving faith is not merely an emotional admiration of Jesus. The five thousand who were fed with barley loaves and a little fish grew enthusiastic over this Galilean and were ready to crown Him as their king. They merely looked upon Him as a miracle man and believed that He as their king could give them an easy and comfortable living, without any effort and work on their part. So there are many today who sing the praises of Jesus of Nazareth because His church and His followers build orphan homes, hospitals, and other institutions of mercy in which suffering humanity finds help and relief. But such outward admiration is not the saving faith.

Saving faith stakes its all on Jesus Christ as the Savior from sin. Such believers in Christ Jesus know that they are hopelessly lost in sin and cannot save their own soul by anything that they do. But they do not despair. Jesus lifts them out of their transgression, and He saves them from the power of sin. This He did when He went to the cross and took upon Himself our obligations and paid the price of our redemption. And He that believeth on Him is saved unto everlasting life. As the drowning man reaches out for a log and holds to it with all the strength that is within him, realizing that this log is the one thing that stands between him and the watery grave, so saving faith clings and holds to Jesus Christ, knowing that He is the One and only One who stands between the sinner and eternal damnation. Jesus becomes the Rock of Ages to which the believer clings.

This saving faith is created by the Holy Spirit

through the Gospel. This faith does not grow of itself. It is not developed by the wisdom of men. That is why the Scriptures say: "By grace are ye saved, through faith, and that not of yourselves; it is the gift of God; not of works lest any man should boast," Eph. 2:8-9.

This faith brings Jesus Christ into our hearts and fills us with hope. Sicknesses and sufferings are trying, but Jesus, as the Lover of our souls and the Keeper of our bodies, watches over us day by day and gives us sufficient strength to carry on with patience and with confidence. Therefore we must trust in Him.

This saving faith brings us at last to everlasting life. There God shall "wipe away all tears," and there shall be "no more pain." Of this Jesus assures us with a double oath, saying: "Very, verily, I say unto you." What Jesus says here is this: "By God, by the eternal God, I say unto you: He that believeth on Me hath everlasting life."

Saving faith, then, looks up to Jesus, the crucified Savior, who shed His holy, precious blood to redeem us lost and condemned creatures that we might be His own.

Prayer

Lord, Thou art ever mindful of Thine own and with a tender love and mercy art holding us in the hollow of Thine hand. Therefore I put all my trust in Thee, certain that Thou wilt be my Strength and Stay. The burdens of my life have been heavy, and my distress is great. Yet Thy loving-kindness has been with me every hour of the day and has kept me through the long watches of the night.

Forgive wherever I have grieved Thee, and by Thy grace cause me to walk with Thee and live to Thy glory. Watch over each one of us in this household and preserve all from every danger of body and soul. Heal me, O Lord, and forgive all my sins, and bring me at last to the glory of that everlasting life which Christ has purchased with His own blood. I ask this for His name's sake. Amen.

Bread and Water

And Jesus said unto them, I am the Bread of Life: He that cometh to Me shall never hunger; and He that believeth on Me shall never thirst. —*John 6:35.*

Bread is the most satisfying food in the world. It is the one staple article used by man in almost every country and nation. Day after day we partake of it and yet do not tire of it. Of other foods, if they are used too often, we sicken. If we had to eat dainty sweets three times a day and nothing else, we at last would become so nauseated that we would refuse them.

Likewise water is used throughout the entire world and refreshes our parching lips at all times.

God in His great wisdom has seen to it that water can be obtained practically everywhere, and it always satisfies.

Jesus tells us that He is the Bread of Life and the Water of Life. What bread and water is to the body, that Jesus Christ is to the soul. Whatever our spiritual needs may be, He satisfies them. There is no condition in life where Christ's presence does not fill us with peace and make us more hopeful and joyous.

Are we troubled with sin? Does our conscience accuse us? At the foot of the cross we find real satisfaction; for there we are cleansed from all our sin through the blood of Jesus Christ. Under the cross we behold sin paid for as our conscience demands, and the heart obtains that forgiveness for which it craves.

Are we troubled with vexing problems? Jesus assures us that He will be with us always. He will guide us as the Good Shepherd day after day. Even though we do not know the way, He does. Even though the future is veiled for us, He sees everything. In the hour of trial He pleads for us at the throne of His heavenly Father. This assurance fills us with hope and gives us real satisfaction.

Are we suffering? Jesus makes easier the burdens of life and daily gives us sufficient strength to carry on. Yes, He comforts us with the promise of eternal life, which He has purchased for us with His own blood. In heaven there shall be no more tears, no sorrows, no pain; for the first things have passed away. In heaven there shall be fullness of joy.

Thus we are certain of one thing, no matter what befalls us: Jesus is the Lover of our soul, the Keeper of our body, our Refuge, and our Friend. He blesses us with His divine forgiveness, He fills us with a glorious hope, He builds up in us faith that will never be shaken. If we come to Him, we shall never hunger or thirst spiritually. He satisfies.

Prayer

Dear Lord, wonderful Savior, I come to Thee in all my weakness and helplessness that Thou mayest take me by the hand and lead me. Guide me with Thine eye into the paths of righteousness, in which I will do Thy will and obey Thy Word. Cleanse me from every sin and blot out of my life my past transgressions through Thy precious blood.

Bless me with cheerfulness and patience. Give me faith and sufficient strength to carry on for today. Keep this household united with Thy holy Christian church and faithful to Thy Word. Protect us from every danger of body and soul. As Thou doest Thy good and gracious will for our welfare here and in eternity, grant us the grace to say with a believing heart: "Thy will be done." Into Thy divine arms of love I place myself with all this household. Amen.

Loaded with Blessings

Blessed be the Lord, who daily loadeth us with benefits.
—*Ps. 68:19.*

Life often is loaded down with troubles and adversities. Many become despondent because of these burdens. After all, we are better off because of these, even though we may not think so.

Burdens steady us. The vessel that is loaded down with freight is in less danger of making shipwreck as it crosses the ocean than the vessel which carries no cargo. The empty boat is tossed to and fro by the storm, while the one loaded down plows safely through the waves toward its destination. Even so it is in life. If we have no responsibilities, no obligations, no duties resting upon us, we easily make shipwreck of faith. Therefore God loads us down with work, with obligations, yes, even burdens us with trouble and pain and adversity.

Looking only at these burdens makes us miserable, wretched, rebellious. But looking to God lightens our burdens and gives us strength. In His Word, God promises to bless us and thus to uphold us as we carry on day after day. Yea, even as we are burdened with trouble, the Lord loads us down with

71

blessings, because of which we should lift up our hearts in praise to Him.

Daily God loads us with His forgiveness. Even though we are weighted down with many problems and hardships, yes, suffering and pain, we receive day after day this greatest of benefits, forgiveness of all our sins.

Daily God gives us bread to sustain and preserve us. In His wisdom He may not give us all that we want—for we might then forget Him—but He does promise us all that we need for the support and wants of the body. And must not most of us confess that He loads us down with an abundance of daily bread? Even in the days of sickness we enjoy many delicacies in food and drink. God is good to us.

Daily God loads us down with strength. We have experienced this in the past and shall do so also in the future. He promises to help us. Often we begin the day thinking that we cannot live through it, but as the evening hours draw nigh, we have received strength and help from the Lord.

God loadeth us with benefits daily. He never leaves us in the lurch. Even though we cannot under-stand all His ways, but look through a glass, darkly, nevertheless we know from His Word that He takes care of us. Therefore we should bless the Lord even on our sickbed, mindful of His many benefits of body and soul.

Prayer

Lord God, who art from everlasting to everlasting, I come in Christ Jesus to Thee as my loving Father, believing in Thy divine love and gracious help. Thou hast been good to me throughout my life, giving me daily bread and Thy glorious Word, which makes wise unto salvation. I have not always appreciated these benefits. Forgive me, O Lord. Remove all my sins in Thy tender mercy. Let me rejoice in Thy forgiveness. I praise Thee because Thou hast blessed me day after day. Thou hast loaded me with many benefits in the past; continue to bless me thus, O Lord.

Above all, grant me steadfastness unto the end for the sake of Jesus, my adorable Savior. Amen.

God's Boundless Grace

For the grace of God that bringeth salvation hath appeared to all men. — *Titus 2:11.*

Life often is considered dirt cheap. Among the Egyptians slaves died like flies. About 100,000 were put to work under the taskmaster's lash to move the huge stones which were lifted into the pyramids. Thousands died from exhaustion, from heat, and from abuse; and nobody cared.

Life is never considered cheap by our Lord. Each and every soul is precious in His sight. Even when man displeases Him by sinning against His holy will, God patiently shows him His grace and love. Even though the Lord must discipline man because of his sinfulness, nevertheless He gives him room for repentance. Before God put Adam and Eve out of the Garden, He promised them the Redeemer, who would deliver them. Even in the days of Noah, God gave the world 120 years of grace. God patiently puts up with the wickedness of man because He considers every soul precious and through His goodness wants to lead all to repentance. Thus the grace of God that bringeth salvation hath appeared to all men.

God's grace is for all. It is universal, excluding none. This universal grace included Adam, who fell from his high estate; David, who committed the dual sin of slaying Uriah and taking his wife; Zacchaeus, who selfishly and greedily robbed the people; Peter, who denied his Lord; the dying thief, who was receiving the just reward of his deeds.

God's boundless grace is even for those who are lost. He passes by none. God's love desired to save Cain, who slew his brother. He was anxious to bring salvation to Esau, who sold his birthright. He was willing to restore King Saul, who had been disobedient time and again. "The Lord is not willing that any should perish, but that all should come to repentance." God's love is boundless.

This grace of God brings salvation. This salvation comes to us in Christ Jesus. God loved the world through Jesus. Since He did not want any to perish, He sent His Son into the world that He might fulfill the Law for us and take the guilt and blame of sin upon Himself and pay the price for our transgressions. From the cradle to the grave Jesus fulfilled the holy will of His Father in thought, word, and deed. By being wounded for our transgressions and bruised for our iniquities He paid for our sins as the justice of God demanded. And this payment satisfied His Father; for He raised Jesus from the dead. By His death and resurrection we are made certain of salvation.

This salvation is brought to us through the Gospel, which is to be proclaimed to every creature. Therefore this grace of God which brings salvation offers *you* forgiveness and eternal life. That is what our text wants to emphasize.

In days of sickness we sometimes feel as though God had forgotten us, as though He did not care that we are in distress. We become discouraged and disheartened when day after day we must endure suffering and pain. Then Satan wants to make us believe that the love of God does not include us. But when the devil comes into our garden and whispers such unholy thoughts, let us again remember that the Lord says in His Word to each and every believer: "The grace of God that bringeth salvation hath appeared to all men." Then say with a believing heart: "This includes also me. God loves me with an everlasting love."

Prayer

O Lord, Thou knowest how weak and helpless I am today. I am in sore straits because of my suffering. Life seems hard as the burdens continue to rest upon me. Yet Thou hast promised, O Lord, that Thy love is for all the sheep of Thy pasture. Therefore I put my trust in Thee. Give me strength to carry on against all odds. Teach me to remember that Thou dost love me with an everlasting love and hast brought unto me salvation through the Gospel, which is for all mankind.

If I have grieved Thee with my worries and my sins, graciously forgive. Teach me to know that Thy grace is boundless and that it is new every day. Open Thou my eyes to see the riches of Thy blessings that are mine even amid my physical distress; for Thou hast given me peace of heart and the hope of eternal life. Thou hast made sure my salvation in Christ Jesus. Give me the grace to live in peace with Thee daily.

Bless our household with this saving faith that we may hold fast to Thee and Thy promises without wavering. I ask this because of Him through whom Thou hast shown Thy love and grace, Christ Jesus, my Lord. Amen.

At the Oak of Mamre

> Then Abraham removed his tent and came and dwelt in the plain of Mamre, which is in Hebron, and built there an altar unto the Lord. . . . And the Lord appeared unto him in the plains of Mamre. . . . And He said, I will certainly return unto thee according to the time of life; and, lo, Sarah, thy wife, shall have a son. —*Gen. 13:18; 18:1, 10.*

Not a great distance from Hebron, in the plains of Mamre, stands an old oak, which is being carefully guarded and protected. Every possible effort is being made to keep it alive. The tree is very, very old. Whether this present tree is actually the same which stood in the plain of Mamre in the days of Abraham it is difficult to say. However, since the Middle Ages this oak has been pointed out as "the Oak of Abraham."

Somewhere near this tree Abraham pitched his tent and built an altar unto the Lord. At Hebron is the Cave of Machpelah, where Abraham is buried with Sarah, Isaac, Jacob, and Leah.

At this oak of Mamre, God made some remarkable promises to Abraham. As the Patriarch sat in front of his tent, the Lord had him look up to the sky and count the stars. God assured him that his descendants would equal in number these stars, although Abraham at the time of the promise was already old and still without a child.

Here at the oak of Mamre the Son of God and two angels visited Abraham, and after the "father of all believers" had broken bread with them, the Angel of the Lord told him that a son would be born to him in his old age. Humanly this seemed impossible. Nevertheless to Sarah and Abraham was born their only son Isaac. God had not failed in His promise.

God is the same faithful Lord today. The promises of His Word are made to you and to me. Sometimes they seem amazingly strange, and we cannot see how they shall be fulfilled. Yet we dare confidently hope that God will keep every one of the promises which He has made to us.

God has promised never to leave nor forsake us. Even though we Christians go into death, our relationship with God does not change. We only change in regard to the present life and are separated from the people who are living in this world. But we are not separated from God; in fact, through death we come into His presence to behold Him face to face.

Again, the Lord has promised to blot out our transgressions and to remember them no more. We have no right to doubt, not even for a moment, that God abundantly pardons. Sin wants to vex our soul; but our heavenly Father assures us that each and every one of our transgressions is removed through the precious blood of Jesus Christ. Thus you and I find peace of heart and mind amid all the changing conditions of life.

God promises to us life everlasting, where there shall be fullness of joy. This fills us with hope. All the suffering and afflictions are but passing. Paul tells us that he considers the suffering of this world rather insignificant and not worth mentioning when he thinks of the glory that awaits us. Remembering these promises of God, we shall be hopeful, confident, and cheerful. These promises outlive even the oak of Mamre.

Prayer

Gracious Lord, I beseech Thee to fill me with a faith like that of Abraham, who amid all the changing scenes of life never questioned Thee nor Thy promises. Thou knowest all things and therefore art acquainted with all my needs. Look upon my affliction and my pain and deliver me out of my distresses. Set my feet upon a rock, and establish Thou my going in and my going out.

Blot out my sins through the blood of my Savior. Bless me with a good conscience and fill me with hope.

Lord, doubts and fears beset me on all sides. Satan whispers that Thy promises have failed. Take me by the hand and lead me. Make me feel secure and safe as the storms of life pass over me.

Make this home a forecourt of heaven, in which Thy Word rules every life and in which each and every one approaches Thy throne of mercy and grace and finds forgiveness and salvation. This I ask for the sake of Him who died that I might live, Jesus Christ, my Redeemer. Amen.

The Door of the Sheep

I am the Door; by Me if any man enter in, he shall be saved and shall go in and out and find pasture. —*John 10:9.*

Prior to my going to the Holy Land I never could quite understand why Jesus in this beautiful lesson on the Good Shepherd calls Himself the "Door of the sheep." There seems to be a mixture of pictures. However, in the Holy Land the shepherd is actually "the door of the sheep." Ofttimes he spreads his legs and lets the sheep pass through them. As each one of the sheep comes to pass through his legs, he stops it for a moment to see if all is well. Should it be bruised, he daubs it with oil. If it looks weary, he refreshes it with cooling water. Thus one by one the sheep enter through the shepherd door and are given individual attention. Having this picture before Him, Jesus says: "I am the Door of the sheep."

Jesus is the Door through which we enter into the spiritual sheepfold. He made the door. He opened heaven, which by the fall of man was closed. Jesus became this Door by meeting the full requirement of the Law, living in perfect obedience to the will of His heavenly Father. Then He paid the price of our disobedience, beginning at Gethsemane and ending on Calvary. By the shedding of His precious blood He has atoned for our sins, made complete payment, and opened the door to heaven.

Through this Door we must enter. We enter it by faith. Now faith is staking your all upon Christ. When a man leaps out of an airplane with a parachute attached to himself, he expects it to open, and he hopes to land safely on the ground. He is staking his all upon the parachute. If it remains closed, he is doomed. So everyone who believes in Jesus feels absolutely sure that He has paid for each and every sin by the shedding of His blood.

Those who enter this Door by faith are saved. They have life. In this world they have spiritual life, and in the world to come they have everlasting life.

Going through this Door, the sheep walk in

safety. The believer has the protection of the Good Shepherd. He protects us against sin, an accusing conscience, and the terrors of death.

The believer also enjoys the divine guidance of the Good Shepherd. Sheep easily go astray. They cannot like other animals scent their way back to the sheepfold. Sometimes it seems as though the Good Shepherd does not take any interest in us, especially when we have misfortunes, long-continued sicknesses, and afflictions.

Here again the Oriental life sheds some light. When a shepherd finds that a sheep is contrary and is persistently straying away from the fold, he deliberately breaks one of its hind legs. Thereafter the sheep cannot walk. The shepherd therefore carries it from place to place, brings it food and refreshing water until the leg has been healed. Shepherds say that a sheep whose leg has been broken and is nursed in this manner will never stray again. I think that the Good Shepherd of our souls sometimes shuts us in through trials and troubles to keep us close to Himself, that we may continue to walk in safety.

Abiding close to the Good Shepherd, we find pasture. This pasture is His Word. This sustains us. This Word is a spiritual food, which nourishes our soul.

Through this Word we are also healed, for it offers us forgiveness of all our sins. We are filled with peace.

This Word comforts us. We are cheered and encouraged through the wonderful promise of the abiding presence of the Good Shepherd.

Come, then, to this divine Shepherd. In His presence you are perfectly secure, you are certain of His continual protection. He guides you day after day and leads you until you reach the heavenly home, where we shall abide in His presence forevermore.

Prayer

O Thou great Shepherd of our souls, who hast laid down Thy life for the sheep and hast brought us into Thy fold, feeding us upon the green pastures of Thy Word and refreshing us with the comforting Gospel, give me grace to follow Thee day by day. In my distress and in my affliction comfort me with Thy Word. In my troubles be Thou my Stay. Strengthen my faith and keep me steadfast. Let me not err or stray away from Thee, who alone canst bring me safely to the eternal home, where all the redeemed will worship and adore Thee forever.

Forgive me, gracious Shepherd, so that my sin may not be counted against me in the Judgment. Wash me whiter than snow. Amen. Praise be to Thee. Amen.

The Comfort of Our Religion

Comfort ye, comfort ye My people, saith your God. — *Is. 40:1*

Our Christian religion chiefly emphasizes the glorious work of Jesus Christ. It tells us that He has come into the world to lift fallen mankind out of sin and to make us heirs of heaven. To do so, He shed His precious blood. This He has done for all the world.

We profess to believe in Jesus Christ. We have accepted the Christian religion. What is the outstanding blessing this Christian faith offers? It may be summed up in one word — comfort. God tells the prophet to comfort the people. There is no one who so readily listens to the Gospel as those who have sorrows and tears, grief and pain. In the crucial moments of life we need more than anything else the comfort of the Gospel.

The Christian religion comforts us when sin haunts and distresses the human soul. Our conscience cannot be silenced by being told to forget about sin. Neither is it satisfied in the long run by doing a good turn a day. One kind deed does not undo the past. Our Christian religion offers something far greater. As the conscience accuses us, we are told that the blood of Jesus Christ cleanses us from all sin.

84

We are assured that not one blot remains. This really comforts, for it tells us that our sin has been paid for as our conscience demands. In Christ we have forgiveness and can be certain that every sin is blotted out.

Our Christian religion comforts us likewise in the hour of trouble. Christian faith does not exempt us from sorrows, pains, and tears. Into Christian homes come sickness, misfortune, and losses. Into some Christian homes come lifelong afflictions. These are things that try our faith. Doubts want to arise in our heart. Satan wants to make us question the goodness and the mercy of the Lord. He will tell us that the ungodly flourish. So we begin to question the justice of God. In such crucial moments God's Word bids us believe that God moves in His mysterious ways His wonders to perform. He promises to be with us so that we need not battle with the problems and the hardships single-handedly. Through His Word He shows us how He has been a present Help in trouble to many of His people and will be to us. This encourages us and comforts us.

In all our trials of body and soul we should go again and again for refuge to the Rock of Ages, Jesus Christ, our Lord. He will never fail us. He will comfort us with the comfort of the everlasting Gospel and send us on our way with cheerfulness and confidence.

Prayer

Lord, gracious Father, I come to Thy throne of grace with heavy heart and with troubled mind. Help me and comfort me in my distress. Thou art my Keeper and hast promised never to leave me. To Thee I lift up mine eyes for guidance and deliverance.

Forgive me all my sins and heal me of all my distress and restore me to health. Bring to my home peace, hope, and joy. Show me that Thy ways are ways of love and mercy through Christ Jesus, my Lord. Amen.

The Olympics of Life

This one thing I do, forgetting those things which are behind and reaching forth unto the things which are before, I press toward the mark for the prize of the high calling of God in Christ Jesus. —*Phil. 3:13-14.*

St. Paul compares life to a race. He is running in the Olympics of life. He lived in an age when the Roman world had its national games at regular intervals. Those who entered the race would carefully train, exercise daily, bathe frequently, and have their bodies rubbed with oil. Everything possible was done by them to make themselves physically fit for the race.

Every Christian is running a race. Should it be

run successfully, we must forget the things that are behind, says the apostle. Which are these things? I find behind me my sins. Unforgiven, they become a real hindrance. Unforgiven, the conscience annoys, tortures, and distresses me. Unforgiven, sin robs me of joy, of peace, and of hope. Many of these sins have not soiled our hands, but they have blackened our heart. They have not disgraced us in the eyes of the world, but they have separated us from God. Unforgiven, sin robs us of heaven.

How can I forget these sins? Only if God remembers them no more. God, however, forgets sin only by blotting them out through the blood of Jesus Christ. I must first come to the cross to have my sins removed. Then I can press forward, forgetting those things which are behind.

I must also forget my grudges if I want to run the race successfully. Not every one has been kindly disposed toward you and me. We have been grieved, our feelings have been hurt. Things have been done which seem unjust and unfair.

But how can we forget that unkind "dig," that unfair slight, that unjust act? Only by forgiving as God forgave us. If we recall the mercies of God, who has blotted out every one of our sins, then the wrongs that have been done to us will fade into insignificance. They will no longer be mountains, but molehills.

I must furthermore forget my worries. Humanly speaking, we have plenty of things to worry about, especially in the days of sickness. But worries are not conducive to health. They hinder the progress of recovery.

But how can I forget these worries? Only by casting them upon the Lord. We must learn in childlike faith to trust in the goodness and in the mercies of God.

Forgetting the things that are behind, we are to reach forth unto the things which are before. "I press toward the mark for the prize of the high calling of God in Christ Jesus." To run the race successfully, we are to live up to our high calling as Christians. We must patiently wait upon the Lord, be mindful of His mercies, live in prayer, and diligently search His Word.

Looking ahead, we shall always keep before our mind's eye the goal, which is heaven. Men and women who are not Christians have nothing to strive for. They simply walk through life, seeking eagerly this joy and that pleasure; but at the same time they are going forward to a dark, dismal eternity. The Christian, however, knows that after the toiling, after the race, after the struggle, there is heaven, where a crown awaits the victor, a crown of everlasting life. Having this in mind, we cannot become despondent, downhearted, and worried in the days of trouble. Full of hope and confidence, certain of victory by the power of God, we shall look forward. Through the grace of our Lord Jesus Christ we shall run the race successfully and in the end reach heaven, our eternal home.

Prayer

Lord Jesus, living Savior, Thou alone standest between me and a hopeless eternity. I thank Thee that Thou hast revealed Thyself unto me and by Thy wonderful grace hast made me Thy child and called me into Thy kingdom. Keep me steadfast unto the end.

Thou knowest the worries and vexations that annoy me. Alone I cannot put up with them. My sins distress me. The worries of the day want to crush me. But I bring all my sins to Thee that Thou mayest blot them out. I bring all my worries and cares to Thee that Thou mayest lift them from my shoulders. Give me the grace to leave all these burdens at Thy feet and to go forward with a new joy and a new hope in my heart.

Bless this home with Thy divine presence, so that we shall not become irritable and unkind. Keep us all in Thy saving grace. I ask this of Thee who hast endured still greater agony and distress on the cross to redeem me, a lost and condemned creature, and to make me Thine own. Amen.

God's Correcting Hand

Looking unto Jesus, the Author and Finisher of our faith; who for the joy that was set before Him endured the cross, despising the shame, and is set down at the right hand of the throne of God. For consider Him that endured such contradiction of sinners against Himself lest ye be wearied and faint in your minds. Ye have not yet resisted unto blood, striving against sin. And ye have forgotten the exhortation which speaketh unto you as unto children, My son, despise not thou the chastenings of the Lord nor faint when thou art rebuked of Him; for whom the Lord loveth He chasteneth and scourgeth every son whom He receiveth. If ye endure chastening, God dealeth with you as with sons; for what son is he whom the father chasteneth not? But if ye be without chastisement, whereof all are partakers, then are ye bastards and not sons. Furthermore, we have had fathers of our flesh which corrected us, and we gave them reverence; shall we not much rather be in subjection unto the Father of spirits and live? For they verily for a few days chastened us after their own pleasure; but He for our profit that we might be partakers of His holiness. Now no chastening for the present seemeth to be joyous, but griev- ous, nevertheless afterward it yieldeth the peaceable fruit of righteousness unto them which are exercised thereby. Wherefore lift up the hands which hang down and the feeble knees and make straight paths for your feet lest that which is lame be turned out of the way; but let it rather be healed. Follow peace with all men and holiness, without which no man shall see the Lord. *Heb. 12:2-14.*

In the days of sickness and trouble we must look to Jesus Christ for help and for guidance. He is the one sure Refuge amid the trials of life. He alone fills us with patience and gives us an understanding heart.

God sends trouble into our lives to chasten or correct us. He does this as our heavenly Father. When a father or a mother corrects the child, this is done because the parent wants the son to grow up as a gentleman. The correcting is not prompted by hatred and dislike. The mother will take time to teach her boy table manners. The father will insist that the lad come home at certain hours in the evening. If he fails to do so, he will be corrected. If he does not listen to the admonition, he will not be permitted to go out at all for the time being.

So God corrects us, not because He hates us, but because He wants us to grow in Christian faith and to develop a Christian character.

Often the son finds these corrections irksome and irritating. If he is not permitted to leave the home on a given evening, he undoubtedly will pout, and the evening will not be the most pleasant in the home.

So likewise we find our afflictions and sicknesses grievous when God sends them into our homes. The burden is heavy; the pain is great; the nights are long. There is no joy as these things are upon us.

In later years, however, the son is grateful as he remembers that his parents were strict and insisted upon discipline. He realizes that these correctings were wholesome and trained him for his lifework.

Likewise we Christians shall behold in the end that our burdens and sicknesses were used by God to discipline us and fit us for life. Therefore we praise Him in later life that He has sent us through the school of sorrows and tears. Through these He has developed our faith and character and saved our soul.

This lesson we shall learn only if we look to Jesus. He is the great Author and Finisher of our faith, who shows us that we must through trials and tribulations enter into the kingdom of God. He endured all patiently and gladly that we might live.

Prayer

Lord Jesus, I come to sit at Thy feet to learn of Thee. Thou didst go to the cross to bear the burden of sin, also my sin, that I might have life and salvation with all the redeemed. As the troubles and afflictions of life press down upon me, be Thou my Strength. Open Thou my eyes to see that Thou art with me. Let Thy divine presence fill me with cheerfulness and patience.

Forgive me where I have sinned against Thee.

Blot out every transgression with Thy holy, precious blood. Fill this household with contentment and teach us to trust in Thee day by day, looking unto Thee as our Savior, as our Helper, and as our Friend. Amen.

Persuaded

For I know whom I have believed and am persuaded that He is able to keep that which I have committed unto Him against that Day. —*2 Tim. 1:12.*

In every age men have lived who wanted to overthrow everything that the Bible teaches and denied that the promises of God made in the Scriptures are true. Some even boldly declare that there is no God and scoff at the idea that the Lord knows everything about me and even is concerned about the troubles which come into my life. Therefore they say that prayer cannot change the order of things and is useless and unnecessary.

Refreshing therefore to the weary mind and to the hungry heart are the positive statements of Paul. Time and again He says: "I know; I am persuaded."

In his old age, as Paul stands at the brink of eternity, he writes to Timothy, his young co-worker, that his faith in his Savior Jesus Christ and in the promises of God is still unshaken. He still believes that the Word of God is eternally true. The promises of God have been fulfilled upon him repeatedly.

"I know whom I have believed." Paul believed in Jesus Christ, God's only Son, our Lord. This Jesus Christ has appeared as Savior and has abolished death and brought life and immortality to light. This He offers through the Gospel. There was not a shadow of a doubt in the mind of Paul that Jesus Christ had redeemed him. He was sure of his salvation, not because he had merited it, not because of his missionary enterprises and efforts, but because Jesus, his Savior, had paid the full price of his redemption. He knew that this Savior would not fail him. Even during the time of his imprisonment and in the hour of death, no matter what would come to pass, he knew that he believed in a Savior who had made his salvation sure.

This same blessed assurance we have. The Gospel, which has been revealed to us, tells us of this Jesus who has come into the world and has overcome sin and death and brought life and immortality to all those who believe. Even in the hours when we are very sick, in great suffering and distress and pain, we still know that Jesus is our Savior. Therefore we trust in Him, holding fast to the Gospel with its glorious promises and its blessed assurance of peace and hope and deliverance.

Paul is persuaded that this Jesus is able to keep that which he has committed unto Him against that Day. That which he has committed unto the Lord is his soul's salvation. When that day comes when he shall appear before the throne, he is persuaded that he shall be received into glory. He has accepted the grace of God in Christ Jesus. That which makes him certain that his salvation is secure is the Word of God, this Gospel of Jesus Christ. This Gospel is eternally true. Therefore every believer can place his soul's salvation in the hands of God. By the power of God we are kept through faith unto salvation.

This is a blessed knowledge and persuasion, especially in the days of sickness and trouble. Satan often whispers that God does not love us. Satan often tries to make us believe that our sins are too many to be forgiven, that our salvation is very doubtful. But if we hold fast to the Gospel, we shall overcome every doubt and all unbelief. Paul, though he confesses himself to be the greatest of sinners, yet tells us that he knows and is persuaded that Jesus Christ through the Gospel has made certain his salvation.

Let us with Paul hold fast to Jesus Christ and be persuaded that He is able to keep us in body and soul day after day. Then joy, peace, and hope will fill our hearts.

Prayer

Gracious Father, I come to Thee with all my burdens and troubles. I ask that Thou wouldst give me strength to quench the fiery darts of Satan, who is ever and again seeking to make me doubt Thy goodness and Thy mercy, Thy promises, and my salvation. Increase my faith and make me more diligent in the study of Thy Word that I may receive from this Gospel peace, forgiveness, hope, and certainty. I place myself in Thy divine hands. Let Thy mercy ever be with me. Teach me to know that Thou dost love me with an everlasting love through Jesus Christ, my Savior.

Watch over each and every one of us and protect us day after day. Teach us to be content. Help us to overcome through our Christian faith every discouragement. Make us patient. We entrust unto Thee our soul's salvation. Keep us in Thy grace and love through Jesus Christ, our Lord. Amen.

No Abiding City Here

Wherefore Jesus also, that He might sanctify the people with His own blood, suffered without the gate. Let us go forth therefore unto Him without the camp, bearing His reproach. For here we have no continuing city, but we seek one to come. —*Heb. 13:12-14.*

Every one of us must find deliverance from sin and the guilty conscience, every one must find comfort amid sorrows and tears, every one must find hopeful assurance as he stands at the open grave if he wishes to escape eternal punishment for his sins, sorrows that will never end, and despair at the sight of death and corruption. The Gospel of Jesus Christ gives us this deliverance, comfort, and assurance. The message of the Cross therefore urges us to build upon surer and safer things than marble, riches, and fame. The Gospel wants us to build for eternity.

We should build for eternity because Jesus Christ has bought us at such a tremendous price. His sacrifice on the cross reveals to us that there must be more than this life; otherwise Christ's agony would be entirely out of proportion. If a firm spends $10,000 for advertising, it must believe the expenditure worthwhile. Jesus Christ sacrificed Himself and went into the depths of hell and was forsaken of God. He, then, must consider the souls of men very precious. There must be a heaven for which He has purchased and redeemed us.

Since Jesus has made such a tremendous sacrifice, we certainly dare not neglect so great a salvation. We dare not ignore eternity. We must build beyond tomorrow and this life.

Every sane and sensible man and woman should build also for eternity because the world really does not want us. This world is greedy, selfish, and unkind. This world is soulless, Godless, and hopeless. This world has no balm for the troubled conscience, no comfort for the sorrowing, and no assurance in the hour of death.

This world does not want the believer. Therefore the sacred writer urges us to go forth unto Christ without the camp and bear His reproach. Every sincere believer by his Christian life and his Christian virtues reproaches the world. The Christian's virtuous life, by contrast, shows up the wickedness of the world.

Therefore the world does not love us. If it does, there is something wrong with us. If the world flatters us Christians, it has an ax to grind with us. For this reason we are not to seek the favors of of the world nor the smiles of the ungodly. Going with the world, we shall die with the world; but living with Christ now, we shall live with Him eternally.

Every sane and sensible man and woman should likewise build for eternity because we have no continuing city here, but seek one to come. No one can deny that all that is earthly fades away. We all must die; if so, why evade the question of eternity? Why should the thought of death be taboo in our lives?

The Bible tells us that there is a bright side to death. Balaam exclaims: "Let me die the death of the righteous, and let my end be like his." Triumphantly Paul exclaims: "O death, where is thy sting?" He comforts the Christians at Thessalonica by saying that their loved ones have fallen asleep in Jesus.

These are strange expressions. They sound like Greek to the worldly minded. But the believer, who builds beyond tomorrow, understands this language. It is sweet music in his ears.

The Christian, thank God, can live and die in peace. He has a glorious heritage through Christ Jesus. He can face the great crises of life and death unafraid. Jesus gives him the blessed assurance that he is redeemed. This fills the child of God with peace and with certainty.

Since we are only sojourning for the time being in this earthly city, it certainly would be unwise to build only for today. What fools we would be if we should neglect our salvation. Let us walk with Christ in this present world, and then we shall live with Him throughout all eternity.

Prayer

Gracious and adorable Savior, I have no other refuge than Thee. There is no other name more precious than Thine. I seek strength in Thee. Thou must be my Help and my Redeemer. Embrace me with Thy love and fill me with Thy divine forgiveness. Let my heart find peace and strengthen my faith with the blessed assurance of eternal life. As all about me fails, let me seek Thee as the Rock of Ages. Turn Thy face toward me in tender mercy and ease my pain and my affliction. Give me the grace to grow day by day in faith and in knowledge of Thee, who alone canst uphold me and comfort me and keep me. Lord Jesus, have mercy upon me and watch over me for today. Grant me Thy peace now and forever. Amen.

Things That God Forgets

But thou hast not called upon Me, O Jacob; but thou hast been weary of Me, O Israel. . . . Thou hast bought Me no sweet cane with money, neither hast thou filled Me with the fat of thy sacrifices; but thou hast made Me to serve with thy sins, thou hast wearied Me with thine iniquities. I, even I, am He that blotteth out thy transgressions for Mine own sake and will not remember thy sins. —*Is. 43:22, 24-25.*

When the Lord wants to impress upon us His lovingkindness and His tender mercies, He compares His love with the love of a mother. He assures us that His love is even greater. "Can a woman forget her

100

sucking child? . . . Yea, they may forget, yet will I not forget thee. Behold, I have graven thee upon the palms of My hands; thy walls are continually before Me." Mothers have abandoned their children, but the Lord never forgets His own.

Neither does the Lord forget His promises. When Jesus, at the close of His ministry, asked His disciples, "Lacked ye anything?" they confessed, "Nothing." God fulfills His promises to man.

Nor does God forget His covenants. To Abraham He said: "Look now toward heaven and tell the stars if thou be able to number them. And He said unto him, 'So shall thy seed be.'" Because of this covenant with Abraham, God preserved His people through the ages until Jesus, the Savior, came.

Thus God keeps His promises and covenants. Yet God forgets. What does He forget? Our text mentions three things: sins, iniquities, transgressions. To sin is to miss the mark. In archery a certain mark is set at which everyone aims. Hitting the center is perfection. God has set a mark for us, telling us in His law what we are to do and what we are not to do. None have attained unto perfection in regard to fulfillment of the Law. Even John confesses: "If we say we have no sin, we deceive ourselves." Every one of us has missed the mark; we have sinned.

God speaks of iniquities, which means turning aside from the straight path. Iniquity is crookedness, something that is wrong or has been twisted. We all have turned aside some time or other from the straight path. The Bible makes no exceptions. We all have been spiteful, hateful, revengeful, unkind, and disobedient.

God speaks of transgressions, which means falling away, omitting to do that which we ought to do. For this reason the Scriptures say: "Therefore unto him that knoweth to do good and doeth it not, to him it is sin." This particular type of wrong is found quite often among Christians. It reveals itself in our indifference to God's Word, our carelessness in worshiping, our lukewarmness, and our coldness. These are things that offend God. They hurt and grieve Him. Therefore you would think that God would remember just these our sins, iniquities, and transgressions. We all know that wrongs are hardest to forget. For this reason we are astounded and filled with amazement to learn that God forgets sins, iniquities, and transgressions.

Why does God forget sins, iniquities, and transgressions? We do not receive this kind consideration because we are deserving of it. The above text is loaded down with charges made against Israel. Their guilt is branded upon them. "Thou hast not called upon Me, O Israel." Prayer life had ceased. Communion with God had been broken. This holds true also today. Our prayers ofttimes cease entirely, or we pray rather mechanically.

Again, Israel is not deserving of God's love for another reason. The Lord says: "Thou hast been weary of Me, O Israel." His people were sick and tired of the Lord. They still performed their religious duties, but they did so with a sigh. They were afraid to give them up entirely, and so they performed them simply to comply outwardly with the divine law. This is an insult to God.

Yes, Israel offended God still more. The Lord says: "Thou hast made Me to serve with thy sins, thou hast wearied Me with thine iniquities." Israel caused the Lord endless trouble and by heaping one iniquity upon another brought distress and vexation to God's heart. We are doing the same thing often. We come to church, and in place of worshiping devoutly we let the devil take the Word from our hearts and say our prayers and creeds thoughtlessly. These sins offend and grieve God.

Yet God forgets. Why? He tells us, "for Mine own sake." Without any worthiness on our part God forgives. His unselfish love for fallen, erring humanity makes Him remember no more our sins, our iniquities, and our transgressions.

How does God forget? "I, even I, am He that blotteth out thy transgressions." God forgets by blotting out. This is done through the blood of Jesus Christ. Clearly the Scriptures declare: "The blood of Jesus Christ, His Son, cleanseth us from all sin."

Jesus blotted out our sins with His holy, precious blood. That is why He was made flesh and dwelt among us. He paid for our sins on the cross. He drank the cup of God's bitter wrath that the Judgment may not come upon us.

Since our sins, iniquities, and transgressions are blotted out, God remembers them no more. This is the promise, "I will not remember thy sins." This is the blessed assurance which comes to us through the Gospel. This is the "glad news" that rings out day after day unto the ends of the earth.

This Gospel is for you and for me. We need this Gospel, especially in the days of sickness and trouble. In such days sins, iniquities, and transgressions come to our remembrance. Our conscience troubles and distresses us. Satan tells us that God is punishing us and exposing our wickedness. What a wonderful relief to know that God has blotted out our transgressions and will not remember our sins! God forgets. This fills us with peace of heart and mind.

Prayer

Lord, Thy loving-kindness and mercy is new every morning. Daily I must come to Thee for cleansing and for healing, for help, and for strength. Thou alone canst blot out all my transgressions with the precious blood of Jesus Christ. Receive me just as I am, unworthy though I be.

Lighten the burdens that rest upon me. Ease Thou my suffering and my pain. Let Thy loving-kindness assure me that Thou hast not blotted me out of Thy remembrance, but only my sins and transgressions. I place myself in Thy divine care. Thou art the Keeper of my body and the Keeper of my soul. Watch over me by day and by night. I ask this for the sake of Jesus, who with His gracious blood has blotted out all my sins and brought me into Thy blessed kingdom, where I find peace and salvation. Amen.

Friends of Jesus

Ye have not chosen Me, but I have chosen you. — *John 15:16.*

The most wonderful gift to the world is Jesus Christ. His friendship is most precious. "Ye are My friends," says Jesus to all believers. Therefore you and I belong to that circle of Christ's friends. By His choice we are His own; for He tells us: "Ye have not chosen

Me, but I have chosen you." We cannot choose Christ as our Friend; for by nature we are dead in trespasses and sins. We have no natural inclination to seek Jesus. We cannot by our own strength come to Him. Being dead, we cannot choose. The stone lying in the quarry cannot choose to be placed into a cathedral or to be carved into a beautiful statue. So we cannot rise out of our spiritual deadness and choose Jesus Christ as our Friend. Jesus must choose us. Jesus has chosen us as His friends at a tremendous sacrifice. While we were yet sinners, He went to the cross to pay the ransom price for our redemption. Had He not atoned for our sins and blotted out our iniquities, we could not be within the circle of His friends. Jesus Himself says: "Greater love hath no man than this, that he lay down his life for his friends." But His love is still greater, He died for His enemies; as Paul says, "Christ died for the ungodly." What a wonderful love and what a tremendous sacrifice by which we are made His friends!

Because of this friendship Jesus keeps open house for us. "Ye have not chosen Me, but I have chosen you. . . . Whatsoever ye shall ask the Father in My name, He will give it you." This gives us the right of prayer. We can enter into the heavenly throne room without formality. To this Friend of friends everyone can come. We can come at all hours of the day and of the night and be certain that He is ready to listen to our prayers.

This friendship of Jesus makes us His confidants. He says: "I have called you friends; for all things that I have heard of My Father I have made known unto you." He has hidden nothing from us. Everything that is necessary to become wise unto salvation He has revealed. He has no court secrets that we do not share. We have a full, complete revelation in the Bible. We cannot expect more. In the Bible He has made known the whole plan of salvation.

This friendship of Jesus makes us children. He says: "Henceforth I call you not servants; for the servant knoweth not what his lord doeth." He embraces us with His love; He clothes us with the garment of His righteousness; He gives us an understanding heart that we may know the truth and gladly follow it. Children! Then also heirs of heaven.

What a privilege to bask in the sunshine of Jesus' friendship! Let us rejoice and be glad that we are His own.

Prayer

Lord Jesus, Thou hast called me out of darkness into the marvelous light of Thy glorious Gospel and hast added me to the circle of Thy friends. Make me steadfast and faithful. If I have grieved and offended Thee, forgive. Remember no more my transgressions. Make my heart a temple wherein Thou dwellest. Give me grace to rejoice in Thee and find delight in walking with Thee.

As the sorrows and troubles of life press upon me, draw nigh and abide with me that I may not fall into unbelief and give way to doubt and despair. Fill me with confidence that Thy promises will be fulfilled also in me. Bless this home and keep us within the circle of Thy friends for time and eternity. Amen.

Christ the Only Way

Thomas saith unto Him, Lord, . . . how can we know the way? Jesus saith unto him, I am the Way . . . ; no man cometh unto the Father but by Me. —*John 14:5-6.*

In the Temple area, in the city of Jerusalem, stands the beautiful mosque known as El Aksa. This, it is claimed, was originally a Christian basilica erected by Emperor Justinian. It was built in the shape of a cross. When the Mohammedans conquered the Temple site, they changed this basilica into a mosque and also changed the form so that the El Aksa no longer is in the shape of a cross.

Not far from the pulpit there are two pillars, or columns, set so close that persons of heavy build can hardly pass between them. The Mohammedans had a saying that any pilgrim who succeeded in squeezing himself through these pillars was assured a place in heaven. In 1881 a devout pilgrim, who was rather obese, endeavored to go through the narrow passage and in the frantic effort died on the spot. For this reason a stanchion, or bar, has been placed between these columns to prevent anyone from passing through this narrow opening.

Man has ever tried by his own efforts to find a way to heaven. Through self-appointed works, by pilgrimages to sacred places, by doing a few good turns a day, many want to earn their salvation. They want to make a claim upon heaven because of their goodness and their uprightness. But not by works of righteousness which we have done can we be admitted to eternal life, because none of us can do enough, or fulfill the holy will of God. If we desire to be saved by the Law, then we must fulfill the Law in every detail and lead a sinless life. This is impossible because we are born in sin. Being born in sin, we also live in sin, and our righteousnesses are as filthy rags in the sight of God, even though we may be the most respectable people in the sight of men. Therefore no one can save himself.

Jesus tells us that there is only one way which leads to the Father. "I am the Way . . . ; no man cometh unto the Father but by Me." Jesus Himself prepared this way with His holy, precious blood. He died on the cross to pay the penalty for our sins as the justice of God demanded. And now in Him and through Him our sins are forgiven as the love of God desires to do. Thus we are saved. This salvation is ours by faith. This faith accepts Jesus as the perfect Savior and puts all its trust in Him as the only Redeemer from sin, death, and the power of the devil. Believing on Jesus Christ leads to heaven. Every other way leads to destruction. There is no other name under heaven given among men whereby we can be saved.

Of this we want to be mindful day after day and build upon nothing else than Jesus and His righteousness. Believing in Him makes sure our salvation and brings untold comfort to us in the days of sickness and affliction, when life seems uncertain and hard.

Prayer

Lord Jesus, Thy blood and righteousness are the glorious dress in which I am clothed by Thy grace to stand before my heavenly Father, redeemed and saved. I am unworthy of this Thy grace; but Thou hast invited me to come just as I am, and therefore I come, O Lamb of God.

Let me experience day by day the joy of forgiveness. Let this spiritual healing give me the blessed assurance that Thou art with me in these days of trouble and art watching over me with Thy tenderest love. Remove from me the worries and cares of the day. Ease my suffering and fill me with cheerfulness and hope.

O Lord, I put all my trust in Thee. Keep me steadfast in the faith that brings me at last into Thy presence throughout all eternity. Be with me now and forevermore, Lord Jesus. Amen.

Taking Things for Granted

They soon forgat His works; they waited not for His counsel. —*Ps. 106:13.*

The sin of ingratitude is quite prevalent. You and I have felt its sting. Have we also realized how often we are guilty of this sin? Are we not taking too many things for granted? We feel that God knows that we appreciate His help and do not take time to thank Him.

"They soon forgat His works; they waited not for His counsel." The Lord's works are mighty. His showers of blessings are many. He is constantly opening His hands and guiding us gently with His eye. Even in the day of sickness He gives us sufficient strength. He surrounds us with good things even when we are afflicted.

Do we appreciate the blessings which remain?

If we do, are we letting God know? The moment things go wrong we hasten to the throne room in prayer. We become impatient and irritable if we do not see immediate results. But after God has answered our prayer, we take little time to thank Him for His mercies.

We take for granted many blessings that are ours even in the days of trouble. We awake in the morning after a restful night and forget to thank God for our peaceful sleep. We breathe the air, we look out upon the beautiful sunshine, we welcome the gentle rain. We behold the starry heavens at night and take all these things for granted. Without price and without money God has given us these things, but we never praise Him for them. All the money in the world cannot buy a beautiful sunshiny day. There is no beauty like the canopy of heaven when at night the millions of stars twinkle.

Above all, we take for granted His mercies and His loving-kindness in forgiving us our sins. He fills us with peace and hope and joy. Seldom we think of thanking God that He has made us wise unto salvation, that He has promised heaven to us as our home.

The sin of ingratitude is severely censured in the Scriptures. The psalmist chides Israel for forgetting the works and the laws of God. God tells us that our neglect is inexcusable. "Hear, O heavens, and give ear, O earth; for the Lord hath spoken. I have nourished and brought up children, and they have rebelled against Me. The ox knoweth his owner and the ass his master's crib; but Israel doth not know, My people doth not consider."

This sin is not only inexcusable, but unreasonable. Therefore Micah exclaims: "Hear ye, O mountains, the Lord's controversy, and ye strong foundations of the earth; for the Lord hath a controversy with His people, and He will plead with Israel. O My people, what have I done unto thee, and wherein have I wearied thee? Testify against Me."

The sin of ingratitude is very prevalent. We need but run through the Scriptures, and we behold everywhere men guilty of this sin. That this sin is prevalent does not make it less sinful. Therefore God warns us in Deut. 8: "When thou hast eaten and art full, then thou shalt bless the Lord, thy God, for the good land which He hath given thee. Beware that thou forget not the Lord, thy God, in not keeping His commandments and His judgments and His statutes which I command thee this day."

You and I have taken many things for granted. We dare not dismiss these neglects with a shrug of the shoulders. As we lie upon our sickbed or are reclining in our invalid chair, we ought to recount the mercies of God and thank Him for those which we still enjoy. Above all we are to remember that God has sent His Son, Jesus Christ, into the world to redeem us. As we daily receive the forgiveness of all our sins, as we daily receive the commonplace blessings, let us not forget to praise God, whose loving-kindness is new every morning.

Prayer

I thank Thee, gracious Father, through Jesus Christ, my Lord and Savior, that Thou hast watched over me again these past twenty-four hours and hast given me strength. Above all I thank Thee that Thou hast forgiven me all my sins, unworthy though I be. Thou hast been so good to me, O Lord, in the past. Thou hast been with me day after day throughout all the years of my life. I have not always appreciated Thy blessings. Today I want to thank Thee, O Lord, out of the abundance of my heart for each and every favor that Thou hast shown me, for Thy continual forgiveness, and for the glorious hope which Thou hast put into my heart through Thy Holy Spirit.

I thank Thee for the loved ones that Thou hast given me, who tenderly take care of me daily. I thank Thee for Thy Word, which has been a source of comfort to me and has driven every doubt out of my heart. I thank Thee that Thou hast established Thy Christian church also in this community and hast given it faithful pastors, who are proclaiming Thy Word, telling of Thy love in Christ Jesus.

Accept my humble praise, O Lord, who hast reconciled me unto Thyself through Jesus Christ, my Redeemer. Amen.

My Savior Lives

He is not here; for He is risen, as He said. Come, see the place where the Lord lay. — *Matt. 28:6.*

Jerusalem and its surrounding territory have many sacred places which are associated with the life and the death of our Lord and Savior Jesus Christ. Jerusalem is a very interesting city. Many who go there today are greatly disappointed, however. The city lacks beauty and charm. Yet everywhere sacred places are pointed out which are associated with the life of our Savior. The legends and the traditions are many. For this reason the people of Jerusalem have become place worshipers. For each and every event in the life of our Lord two places, as a rule, are pointed out, each contending for the honors. Thus there is a Church of the Holy Sepulcher within the city wall and likewise Gordon's Tomb outside the Damascus Gate. So each and every one who makes a pilgrimage to the Holy Land may choose one or the other, according to his fancy, as the place where our Lord was buried and from which He rose from the dead. We therefore cannot like the first disciples come and see the place where the Lord lay.

It matters very little today as to which of the two places is the actual tomb of our Lord; indeed, most likely neither is the place where the Lord lay. However, it is of the greatest importance that we know that Jesus is not among the dead, but that He rose from the dead and that on the third day the tomb, wherever it may have been, was empty. We have a risen and living Savior. Someone has inscribed over the entrance of the gate leading to Gordon's Tomb the words of our Lord: "I am the Resurrection and the Life." We are to know and believe that Jesus is risen from the dead.

Nothing is more comforting than to know that the tomb is empty and that Christ is risen. This fills us with peace; for it gives us the blessed assurance that Christ has accomplished His work of reconciling us to the Father and has purchased for us forgiveness of all sins with His holy, precious blood.

The fact that the tomb is empty fills us with an undying hope, the hope that this our mortal body shall rise again from the dead to be like unto Christ's glorious, resurrected body. Heaven, therefore, is to be our eternal home.

That the tomb is empty takes away every uncertainty. If Christ is risen, then He is the Son of God, and all that He has said and promised is gloriously true. Our salvation is made certain through the resurrection of Jesus Christ from the dead.

Knowing this, we can bear the trials and tribulations of life with greater ease. We know that they are but of short duration, and after the sorrows and sufferings, the toilings and afflictions, comes the eternal joy of heaven. We know whither we are going because Christ rose from the dead.

Prayer

Lord Jesus, risen Savior, I rejoice that Thou hast come forth out of the tomb as Victor over sin, death, and the devil. Thou hast crushed the Serpent's head and hast been recognized as the triumphant Conqueror by our heavenly Father. Because Thou dost live, I, too, shall live according to Thy promise. As living Savior abide with me day after day. I believe that Thou art with me always, according to the blessed assurance given to Thy people. Grant that Thy unseen presence in our home may fill me with hope and peace and cheerfulness.

Lift Thou my burdens and lighten my suffering. Above all, forgive me all my sins and bless me with a faith which will never doubt Thy promises. Bring me at last with all this household to the everlasting mansions to share with Thee the glory of eternal life. Amen.

My Savior Ascends

And while they looked steadfastly toward heaven as He went up, behold, two men stood by them in white apparel, which also said, Ye men of Galilee, why stand ye gazing up into heaven? This same Jesus which is taken up from you into heaven shall so come in like manner as ye have seen Him go into heaven. – *Acts 1:10-11.*

We have become very much earthbound. In our everyday life heaven seems rather far away. The Christians of the first century greeted one another with "Maranatha!" which means, "The Lord is coming." They were daily expecting the return of Jesus.

Jesus has brought heaven near to us. He has bought heaven for us with His own precious blood. To His disciples He said: "In My Father's house are many mansions; if it were not so, I would have told you. I go to prepare a place for you. And if I go and prepare a place for you, I will come again and receive you unto Myself that, where I am, there ye may be also."

To this heaven Jesus ascended after His resurrection. Before He ascended, He gave a commission to His people to go and preach the Gospel to every living creature. This Gospel offers us forgiveness of sins, reconciliation and peace with God, comfort in the day of trouble, and the hope of eternal life. The purpose of the Gospel is to save. As long as we are in this world, we Christians should hear this Gospel and tell others of the hope that is within us.

Jesus ascended blessing His followers. Because of this blessing the gates of hell shall not prevail against the church, and the Gospel shall be preached unto the end of days to fill us with the blessed assurance of Christ's help. At times we become discouraged because the journey is hard. We meet with disappointments, with sickness, and with sorrow; but Christ assures us of His divine blessings. He upholds us and brings us safely to the eternal mansions.

Christ ascended, assuring to us His abiding presence. Even though we do not see Him, He is with us. He has said: "Lo, I am with you alway, even unto the end of the world."

Christ ascended visibly and bodily. He is a living Savior who with tender love and mercy watches over His loved ones.

Where did Jesus go? He ascended into heaven to sit at the right hand of God the Father Almighty. Therefore He is ruling over the world as King of kings. Above all, He is the Shepherd and Head of His Christian church and is protecting its members. The church shall remain unto the end of days. He is ruling over the redeemed as the Lamb that was slain and now liveth.

How will Jesus come again? He will come as He went. He will come visibly. He will come as true God and true man. He will come to judge the quick and the dead, raise all from the dead, and take all believers into His eternal kingdom.

Is there room in heaven for me? There is much room in heaven. The multitude of those who are redeemed is so great that no man can number them. But there is room in heaven for those only who have been made clean in the blood of the Lamb, who have accepted Jesus Christ as their Savior from sin and as their Lord and God.

Prayer

Lord Jesus, to Thee I look for peace and hope and certainty. Amid my trials and sufferings I come to Thee; for Thou art my Strength and my Help. Amid my distress keep before mine eyes heaven, which is promised to the people of God. Let me not become discouraged and disheartened as I journey through life amid its sorrows and tears. Teach me day after day to know that the sufferings of this world are not worthy to be compared with the glory that Thou hast prepared for us in Thy eternal kingdom.

Keep us all, gracious Savior, faithful to Thy church. Let nothing be dearer to us than Thy Word of Reconciliation. Let not the pleasures of this world nor the cares of this life nor the sufferings of this body blind us to the glories of heaven. Grant that we may all stand at last before Thy throne as Thy redeemed and saved to praise Thee, the Lamb upon the throne, the King of kings, and the Lord of lords. Amen.

Serving the Lord on the Sickbed

Confined to our home, we ofttimes think that we can do nothing. Yet even as invalids we can serve our Lord and do this day after day.

We can count our blessings. Yes, even in the days when we are ill, are suffering, are in pain, God is showering His blessings upon us. This David recognizes when he says in the 103d Psalm: "Bless the Lord, O my soul, and forget not all His benefits; who forgiveth all thine iniquities; who healeth all thy diseases; who redeemeth thy life from destruction; who crowneth thee with loving-kindness and tender mercies; who satisfieth thy mouth with good things." The Lord daily forgives us our sins; He surrounds us with loved ones; He gives us strength to carry on day after day; He provides for us tasty food; He comforts us through His Word. These are blessings that we are enjoying even in the days of sickness and helplessness. Let us recognize these blessings and thank God.

We can pray. Prayer is a heart-to-heart talk with God in which we make all our wants known to our heavenly Father, who has given us His Son, Jesus Christ. Our prayers are like letters to friends and loved ones, telling God everything that is happening in our life. We are to pray for the church, for individuals who are still without, for friends who are growing cold and indifferent to the Word, for the missionaries who are laboring in foreign fields, for anyone whom we know to be discouraged and disheartened.

We can praise the Lord. Paul sang praises to God in prison. Amid his trials and troubles he was cheerful and hopeful. Every Christian can sing to the Lord because God fills his heart with an undying hope, the hope of eternal life.

We can read. God has given us the Book, His revelations, which make us wise unto salvation, which comfort us in trouble, which help us overcome our doubts and misgivings. This Book we dare not ignore, especially since Jesus Himself tells us: "Search the Scriptures." These Scriptures are "profitable for doctrine, for reproof, for correction, for instruction in righteousness." These Scriptures speak to us day after day and have invaluable lessons for us.

Thus we can fill the day doing things to the glory of our God and fill our hearts with peace and with joy in the Lord.

Prayer

Lord God, Thou hast made a covenant with me in which Thou hast promised to be my gracious Father and I Thy redeemed child through Jesus Christ. Therefore I seek Thee for strength and help, for Thou art able to save unto the uttermost. I ask Thee to continue to be with me today with Thy love, with Thy divine forgiveness, and with Thy help. Fill me with the joy of service and teach me to know that I can live to the glory of Thy name even when confined to my sickroom. Preserve me from discontent. Bring to my remembrance the great suffering and agony of my Savior, who has gone to the cross to redeem me that I might be Thine own. Give unto me peaceful days and restful nights. Bless this household with Thy divine presence and keep us all in that saving faith which is in Christ Jesus, my Lord. Amen.

TEACH ME TO PRAY

Prayer While the Family Is at Church

Lord, gracious and merciful, bless Thy Word today on all who are assembled at Thy house. Remove every distracting thought and all impenitence that Thy Word may find room in each and every heart. Strengthen and awaken in us faith in Thy Son Jesus Christ, our Savior and our Lord. Amen.

Morning Prayer

I thank Thee, heavenly Father, through Jesus Christ, my Savior, for watching over me this night. I ask Thee graciously to be with me today, protecting my body from all dangers and guarding my soul from the snares of sin. Strengthen my faith and keep me steadfast unto the end. Give me the grace to walk with Thee and to serve Thee. Let Thy holy angels surround me that Satan and sin may have no power over me. Amen.

Evening Prayer

I thank Thee, heavenly Father, gracious and merciful, that Thou hast been with me throughout the day. Blot out through the precious blood of Jesus Christ every sin which I have done this day in thought, word, and deed. Mercifully protect me this night that no harm nor danger may befall me. Therefore I place myself into Thy hands, my body and my soul, asking that Thou wouldst send Thy holy angels to watch over me. Protect all those who trust in Thee and bring me at last with all the redeemed to the eternal day in heaven. I ask this for Jesus' sake. Amen.

Prayer Before Meal

Lord God, heavenly Father, Thou hast opened Thine hand and blessed us with this daily bread. Grant that we may receive it from Thy bountiful hands with thanksgiving; through Jesus Christ, our Lord. Amen.

Prayer After Meal

We thank Thee, gracious Father, for these Thy gifts, which we have enjoyed through Thy bountiful goodness in Christ Jesus, our Lord. Amen.

Daily Bible Readings for Shut-ins

Readings from the Life of Our Lord and Savior Jesus Christ

1. Luke 2:1-14
2. John 1:1-14
3. Matthew 2:1-12
4. Luke 2:25-38
5. Matthew 2:13-23
6. Luke 2:41-52
7. Matthew 3:13-17
8. Matthew 4:1-11
9. John 2:1-12
10. John 3:1-21
11. Luke 5:1-11
12. Matthew 5:1-16
13. Luke 11:1-13
14. Luke 15:11-24
15. Luke 7:36-50
16. Matthew 9:18-26
17. Mark 10:13-31
18. John 11:1-44
19. John 15:1-16
20. Luke 18:31-43
21. Matthew 21:1-11
22. John 13:1-20
23. Luke 22:21-38
24. John 17:1-26
25. Luke 22:39-53
26. Luke 22:54-62
27. Luke 23:1-25
28. Luke 23:26-45
29. John 19:25-42
30. Mark 16:1-20
31. Acts 2:1-47

Readings from the Prophets

1. Isaiah 40:1-11
2. Isaiah 40:26-31
3. Isaiah 1:16-20
4. Isaiah 5:1-4
5. Isaiah 6:1-8
6. Isaiah 9:1-7
7. Isaiah 35:3-7
8. Isaiah 41:8-10
9. Isaiah 42:1-8
10. Isaiah 43:22-28
11. Isaiah 44:21-23
12. Isaiah 49:13-16
13. Isaiah 52:7-10
14. Isaiah 53:1-9
15. Isaiah 53:10-12
16. Isaiah 54:7-13
17. Isaiah 55:1-11
18. Isaiah 60:1-6
19. Jeremiah 17:9-14
20. Jeremiah 23:21-24
21. Jeremiah 29:7-13
22. Jeremiah 31:31-37
23. Ezekiel 3:17-21
24. Ezekiel 34:26-31
25. Daniel 6:1-9
26. Daniel 6:10-17
27. Daniel 6:18-28
28. Joel 2:28-32
29. Micah 7:16-20
30. Malachi 3:1-6

Choice Readings from Proverbs

TEXT INDEX